Victory
one moment at a time

Unlocking the Power of the Master Mind

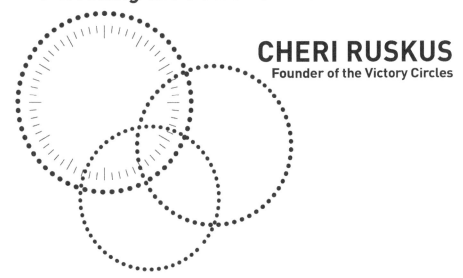

CHERI RUSKUS
Founder of the Victory Circles

MORGAN JAMES PUBLISHING • NEW YORK

Victory
one moment at a time.

ISBN: 978-1-61448-082-2 (Paperback)
    978-1-61448-083-9 (eBook)
Library of Congress Control Number: 2011934469

Published by:
MORGAN JAMES PUBLISHING
1225 Franklin Ave Ste 32
Garden City, NY 11530-1693
Toll Free 800-485-4943
www.MorganJamesPublishing.com

Interior Design by:
Rachel Lopez
rachel@r2cdesign.com
Interior Graphics by:
Maddy Hopkins
MNHopkinsDesign.com

In an effort to support local communities, raise awareness and funds, Morgan James Publishing donates one percent of all book sales for the life of each book to Habitat for Humanity.
Get involved today, visit **www.HelpHabitatForHumanity.org.**

Also by Cheri Ruskus

The Victory Letters – Inspiration for the Human Race

For more information on how to further apply the
Master Mind Principles to your life and business
Get the *Victory One Moment at a Time Action Guide*
at **www.VictoryCircles.com**

Do not take this moment lightly for it is the most important moment of your life –
it is all there is of the present. Live it to the fullest for it will never come again.

All that has gone before it is a memory and all that will come after
it is only a hope or dream of future things.

It is more than the beginning of tomorrow and the end of yesterday. Make it
a great moment, it is your life right now and you will never live it again!

~Jeannine Landreau

This book is dedicated to my loving mother, Jeannine Landreau, the strongest woman I have ever known. Your memory will now be a precious part of my every moment.

And to my daughter, Bailey Jeann. As you strike out into the world to become all that you can be… never forget to dream big while enjoying each moment along the way.

The biggest loss of not living in the moment is this moment.

~Cheri Ruskus

TABLE OF CONTENTS

CHAPTER 6: Victory… And a pleasing personality 121

Bringing Forth the Best of Your Unique Features and Strengths

CHAPTER 7: Victory… And Accurate Thinking 141

Finding Clarity in Your Thoughts, Decisions and Beliefs

INTRODUCTION

Victory One Moment at a Time

A mind troubled by doubt cannot focus on the course to victory.

~Arthur Golden

One thing is certain in this human life that we lead… the only aspect that we are really guaranteed is this very moment of time. I had originally entitled this book, **Victory One Day at a Time**. In the throes of bringing it together, I realized that it's not just the days that bring us our victories, but also all those special cumulative moments, from watching a butterfly flutter across our path to something as miraculous as watching our child walk across the stage at their high school graduation.

We have come to a place in time where we are always trying to do more and be more. Then there is our business life, that "keeping a roof over our head" piece of our work life, which can easily turn into passion. Success lies in enjoying our work as much as our play, when in fact our work becomes our play. I am a huge proponent of this and am grateful to be able to claim it to be true for me.

While we can and should plan for things to come, we should also not forget to enjoy and celebrate the victory of life itself – every single moment. Nearly ten years ago I decided to bring a lifelong dream to fruition. I had always wanted to be a writer but was not sure how. So I tossed out the idea of writing the next great American novel and decided to start small and write from my heart. For me, it initially came out in the form of something I called, *The Victory Letter*. It was a reminder for me to write at least once a week about the things that mattered to me most in my life, my little victories. I had decided to send it out on Monday mornings, the one day each week that we all seem to need a little extra jump-start.

What I found was the people who received this email letter every Monday in their inbox were responding. The things I felt, they felt. I was touching a nerve that started me on a path to continue writing and connecting with others. These were both men and women who were here in my own back yard in Boulder, Colorado as well as in various nooks and crannies across the country.

This book before you is a culmination of the ideas that were brought up in those letters. It also incorporates with them the Master Mind principles that have unfolded through my creation of the *Victory Circles*, Master Mind forums for women entrepreneurs. You may have heard the term mastermind before but may still not be clear on exactly what that is, our why it might be important to you. This work was inspired by the mastermind principles first penned by Napoleon Hill. Mr. Hill was probably the first "motivational" person who came into my life back in my early twenties. His book, *Think and Grow Rich*, planted ideas in my head that I had never thought about before.

I have opted to make this term, *mastermind*, two words instead of one to pay homage to the mastery of our minds. A Master Mind is when a like-minded group comes together on a regular basis for the overall success of everyone in the group. Over the course of the last several years I have had the privilege to create the Victory Circles with like-minded women entrepreneurs who continuously are fine-tuning the making of their business dreams and aspirations, making them into realities. They have thrown fear into the backseat of their car as they pursue their passions. We meet on a monthly basis to share and celebrate our individual and collaborative victories. Along with acknowledging our victories come the realties of the many facets and components of lives and businesses that need to be fine-tuned. The key is that these women are taking the time to fully pay attention to every aspect of their business.

In this book you will find 11 of the 17 principals for success that Mr. Hill outlined in his book, **Laws of Success**. Keeping in mind that Mr. Hill wrote these in the early 1900's I have updated certain aspects of the principals to further assist the entrepreneur of today. I have also added one more principle, creating a habit around the element of self-control in saving time by honoring time. This gives us the twelve Master Mind principles for success that we have come to utilize in the Victory Circles.

There is a small sign I have hanging over my desk asking the question, *"Is this really the way I ought to be spending my precious time on earth?"* This is my own wake-up when I start to fall asleep at the wheel of my life. What is yours?

Every morning we look in the mirror and see our own unique face looking back. It is during this time that each of us has the opportunity to realize all the gifts we have already been given. No matter where each of us is currently in our life, we can stop and take the opportunity of that moment each day to evaluate our journey and to discover the unwrapping of our purpose. Victory does not have to mean you have a fan club or are adorned with fancy things in your life. It is, again, remembering even the simple things like the ability to breathe each day while having those we love, care for and admire breathing right along with us.

During the course of the past three years I had the life-changing experience of having my beloved mother diagnosed with ovarian cancer. During the course of writing this book, she said her eternal goodbye after contracting Leukemia – created by the chemo treatments. Sadly, it was the cure that ended up taking her from us.

As with anyone who has experienced a family member diagnosed with cancer, it makes you stop to catch your breath and realize priorities. Somehow cleaning out your inbox, getting the house clean, and dealing with all your to-do's don't seem as important. Your thoughts are on praying and believing that the one you love so dearly will prevail and overcome the disease.

Though my mother fought the good fight, she did not prevail – but she lived life to the fullest all the way up to the end. It was a huge wake-up call and realization of the fragility of life. The experience, and life now without her have reminded me that my purpose is to get out there and <u>be</u> more, not necessarily always doing more. There seems to be a growing trend in our society today that keeps us moving, moving, moving. To Do lists get longer while time to spend doing what we really want to do gets shorter. My hope is this book will help you to stop filling up your calendar to the boiling over point and fully engage with the people and essences in the life you have been given.

So here is the format for the book: Each chapter addresses an essential Master Mind principle, followed up by a number of individual Victory Letters that have been pulled from my collection over the years. These letters will give you a deeper understanding of the principles through thoughts and life examples. The important factor to keep in mind is that this book is designed not be read through from cover to cover in one sitting. It is not a rolling story but in fact glimpses of moments of my life. Of course, read it how you like, remembering to pick it up and read it when you are looking for inspiration. Grab a key element from a chapter that catches your attention and think it through, thinking about how it applies in your life and in your business right now…in this moment.

There are many things that inspire us to do what we do each day. A big part of my inspiration is my immediate family. My husband, Ed, and my two children, Travis and Bailey, are mentioned throughout. They are the fuel to my fire and passion. When I started writing the letters the children were 11 and 9. Today they are almost 21 and 19 with Travis in his third year of college and Bailey embarking into her first year. You will meet them through the course of the Victory Letters as the years and seasons change.

The other daily constant in my life is my special dog Samantha, a beautiful and kind yellow lab whose spirit has solidly filled the essence of our family. A recent addition to our family is a puppy named Isabella or Izzy for short. As I write, they both are usually curled up at my feet, inspiration in itself. It is my hope that the combination of the Master Mind principles and the Victory Letters will assist you in finding many successes and victories along your way!

Cheri Ruskus

Niwot, Colorado

June, 2011

Victory...
And the Entreprenuer

The Power of the Master Mind
and Defining a Definite Chief Aim

I climb, I reach, beyond my dreams,
Knowing what I can do.
The fame, the glory of what's to come,
To walk in my own shoes.
To not look back with regret or shame,
To hold my head up high,
To know I've done all I can do,
Reaching farther than just to try.

1

Can you remember the first time you ever felt the heartbeat of a business? Not just any business, but your business, the one you created with your own sweat and tears. You know—that feeling you get when your ideas grow into a viable business as the adrenaline producing flow of customers coming and going, phones ringing and the achievement of putting commerce into action. That yearning was instilled in me at a young age, and I have never lost it. Business is my passion.

My first entrepreneurial stirrings came to life at the restaurant of my Aunt Norma. As a child I couldn't wait to get to her place to "play" business. There was an energy that she and my cousins created (not to mention great home-cooked food) that brought to life an excitement in me every time I went there to visit.

Geographically though, we lived just far enough away that it would not become a reality for me to become a part of her restaurant. What I was able to do though, was make believe that I was, and in fact I used her as a reference for my first "real" job. She came through for me with flying colors! The job was at a mom and pop hamburger stand, near my high school during my freshman year. I remember so well being shocked when they called me to tell me that I had the job. Thanks Aunt Norma!

The first day on the job I was pretty scared, because I really had no restaurant experience, showing up for work as green as I could be. Turned out my new boss, a New Yorker transplanted to Southern California, was a bit "grumpy" shall we say. But I bit the bullet and every day I would rush from school and take over the order window, learning that their business meant working fast and furiously inside a small window of time. On came the high school kids on their lunch break from school, the same kids who were my peers just moments before I showed up for work.

As I wrote the orders Lou would bark at me about my writing clarity (or lack thereof). It was a crazy hour and a half of true mayhem each day. As time passed Lou actually started to like me as well as my work performance. Perhaps the first time I ever felt a sense of accomplishment was when he called me into his office, a 9 x 9 storage room. Totally ready to be chewed out for something,

I discovered that he decided to surprise me instead. He shared with me that for my hard and consistent work, he was promoting me to the position of Night Manager. Wow, a promotion, a sense of accomplishment and actually being appreciated. While it came with only a 10 cent an hour raise I was elated. This was my first business victory!

While a move to live with my father ended my Hamburger Diva Night Manager position, the job filled me with the growing knowledge and confidence that I could do good work. During my high school years I bounced around a bit looking for "the" job I would enjoy the most. While living in Central California with my father I did some very labor-intensive jobs including packing oranges and peaches (the itchiest job I ever encountered). Deciding that I missed working with customers during my senior year of high school I went to work at a retail women's clothing store.

I can say, looking back all these years later that each job I held allowed me to find a bit of myself, yet left me wanting to find out more. With no funds available for college I opted to go straight into the working world, full time. Perhaps not the best decision, but the one I made.

It's funny, in writing these words Frank Sinatra's voice comes into my head singing *My Way*. You know the tune… *"Regrets, I've had a few but then again too few to mention. I did what I had to do, saw it through without exemption."*

The academic path I took was to the School of Hard Knocks. Yes, initially in my young adult life, I educated myself through Real World 101, finding people to surround myself with who could educate me and show me the light. Looking back, it seems that once a company quit teaching me and the work became robotic, that's when I would seek greener pastures. Work has always been for me much more than just a "paycheck."

Passion is why I became an entrepreneur. My businesses along the way have become very much a part of my heart and my spirit, especially when I know that I am helping others to be all that they can become – from my employees to my customers. Interestingly enough, my first "real" business at the age of 27 was working with other entrepreneurs by helping them answer their telephones.

While they were out doing their business or tending to their personal lives my first company, Business Answers, was more than just the average answering service. In fact, we fully represented our clients company remotely via the inbound telephone calls that were re-routed to our office. I really loved it! They say you should not fall in love with your business, but I did for nearly 16 years.

Initially my entrepreneurial "empire" was a small, shared office space with a woman who ran a secretarial service. Even though I found myself answering telephones sometimes 12 hours a day, in very cramped quarters, I really loved it. It was all mine. I was making a nice living creating my own reality. I loved my customers and they loved me. Life was good.

The constant change in technology in the late 80s and 90s allowed for many business possibilities. I married, had children, and my husband and I bought a commercial building to house the business. Eventually the business would have a staff of 12 as we expanded the services to encompass the many needs of our small-business clients.

One thing is for sure, when you own a business there are many ups and downs, good times, bad times, and times in between. The key I found that kept my flame burning was to insure the flame was burning at all times and not to allow myself to get bored or burned out. For me, I found that if there was an opportunity to grow and learn every day it charged me and put me in the "zone."

At various times I have learned from my clients and sometimes from vendors and sometimes from the most unexpected places. The key is to continue to learn. It is that passion to learn, I believe, that led me down the road to become a Business Coach. As someone who thrives on assisting others in making their business dreams come true, watching the entrepreneurial flame in the eyes of another is exciting and so very gratifying.

What I have also found to be true is that the more you surround yourself with the support of others – the more you will find success. When I was out there in the world doing the typical meet-and-greet networking I actually did feel quite alone. Not seeing another alternative to the same old, same old in the local marketplace, I did what any good entrepreneur would do… I decided to create my own by combining the relationship building aspect of networking, mixing it with support, and a whole lot of inspiration.

Taking my experience as a business woman, my coaching skills and my love for the entrepreneurial dream, in March of 2006, I created the first Victory Circle Master Mind group. Once again in my life this venture allowed me to be part of something bigger than myself. All the while allowing my own individualism to shine through – as any good entrepreneurial venture should.

As I write the words for this book I am in the beginning phases of launching the Victory Circles on a national level inviting Business Coaches from across the country to join us as Victory Circles Facilitators. This new phase is fully engaging my passion to assist even more entrepreneurs than I could do single handedly and to create a place to come for support and inspiration. Having this happen with other like-minded individuals who share similar passions has been such a winning combination.

Here is where the Master Mind principles, which were first laid out by Napoleon Hill in his *Laws of Success* came fully into play in my life. Through the course of this book we will focus on the 12 primary principles that I have chosen as being most important for today's entrepreneur and how they can help you to move forward in business and in life. The principles bring to light all the key elements necessary for having your business fill your heart and soul as you move towards success and filling your bank account.

The first critical aspect of participating in a Master Mind is being open to the idea of consistently working with an ongoing group of like-minded individuals (no less than three no more than 12). As you open your mind to the possibilities of moving your business forward, you will also be listening to the wants and needs of the other entrepreneurs in the circle. This "sharing" will allow each person in the Master Mind to gain insights to each others joys, pains, challenges and insights that exist for them in their business today. The key is to have this process be an open forum of trust, resulting in productive feedback that is based on each member's experiences and expertise in business.

With the proper group of people in place, you, the individual entrepreneur, needs to put a good deal of focus and attention into the first principle of the Master

Mind, which is being able to define your Definite Chief Aim. This is the why, the what, and the how of where you are going in your current entrepreneurial venture. In the Master Mind environment you cannot assist another if you yourself aren't fully clear on where it is you are going with your own business.

In order to understand your unique Definite Chief Aim, you need to ask yourself the question, what does it really mean to find victory in your business life? Is it the amount of money you make, the work that you do day in and out, or the difference that perhaps you make in the world? In other words, what is it that brings the tick to your tock?

There are proven statistics that people who retire with nothing on their horizon but fishing and golfing live shorter lives. Why? Perhaps, the answer lies in the fact that they have lost a strong definite purpose in moving forward in their life. The lack of passion and moving towards something with a deep meaning, defined by you and you alone, can leave you without a sense of purpose and the excitement to pop out of bed every morning. Yes, life can simply become dull and uneventful. This of course can never be possible if you want to be at the helm of a thriving and successful business.

If you have been contemplating fully jumping into the entrepreneurial arena but have found yourself hesitating, ask yourself why. Not enough money or time? Perhaps you are lacking the conviction of your idea or missing pieces to the idea that will bring it to fruition? You could also simply have so much fear wrapped around the possibility of failing, of falling flat on your face, that you have stopped yourself from your destined path. Just remember they are all excuses – if you really… really want to make the dream of your business happen, you indeed can.

If you are currently running your own business and have lost your passion, your mojo, there is no time like the present to find out why. A Business Coach can indeed assist you in fully understanding what it is that is stopping you. Go out, get the ongoing support you need and to get it back! This could mean restructuring your business, adding new components – or even getting out of your current business to start one that fully encompasses the strengths and passions that you possess.

Great stories of people climbing up from nothing or rebuilding from the ashes are what the halls of great businesses are built of and from. Perhaps Steve Jobs (one of my entrepreneurial heroes) summed it up best when he said,

> "I'm convinced that about half of what separates the successful entrepreneurs from the non-successful ones is pure perseverance."

The following Victory Letters bring to light the essence of being an entrepreneur and how connecting with your own and others entrepreneurial spirits can be the fuel to the untapped fire within you, leading you towards greater success. Open up your mind to your possibilities as you look past what has always been right in front of you. Delve deeper into the potential of being all that you can become. As you begin to get your arms around this process called the *Master Mind* and mastering your own business, begin to look closely at how you define your *Definite Chief Aim*.

The Water's Edge

My life is like a stroll on the beach, as near to the edge as I can go.

~Thoreau

Happy Monday,

Can you almost hear the crashing of the surf from this morning's quote?

Can you imagine the sand between your toes as you stand next to the water's edge?

It sounds so divine to me this morning as I begin to plan for my week ahead.

Have you ever wondered how close to the water's edge you could go? And sometimes, all it takes is getting your feet wet to enjoy the possibilities of going into the water a little bit further.

This past Friday I had a lovely lunch with a friend and coaching colleague of mine, Cynthia. We were originally celebrating her courageous decision to head to Italy and points beyond in the next few weeks so that she can explore the possibilities of that shore. I was intrigued and amazed by her ability to put her life here in Colorado on hold as she takes at least six months for this journey in discovering a deeper part of herself.

She shared with me during our lunch that she had also just agreed that morning to work with an agent who would help her in getting a publisher for her book. Anyone out there who is a writer knows how huge this is and we had plenty of reason to celebrate over our lunch. As we munched on our food and sipped our celebratory glass of wine, I was touched by how much her being on this planet has meant to me in my life. She was a key person in assisting me to get my writer's groove on many years ago! She has made a big difference in my life! It will be wonderful to hear of her journeys.

So, you might have guessed it – some questions are coming your way – How close to the water's edge do you allow yourself to get? Once you get there how often do you allow your feet to get wet? And even further still – how often do you fully dive into the water of life – letting it fully embody all of who you are?

As I happily began to turn the soil in my garden yesterday (it was a spectacular day here in Colorado), I pondered those questions. I realized that for me, I usually need a good dose of empowerment to get me beyond the shore – as most of us do. Take a look at the word empowerment and decide where in your world you are currently standing.

E - Entrepreneurial Spirit Engaged, allowing you to go where you need to go.

M - Masterminding with like-minded people whose goals reflect your own.

P - Prioritizing what is really important to you today and tomorrow.

O - Organizing your time, effectively getting you where you need to go.

W - Winning at what you do each day, no matter the simplicity or complexity.

E - Enlightenment, keeping learning fun, light and mandatory.

R - Reinventing yourself to be whatever it is that you want to be.

M - Mentoring others as you continue to engage with mentors of your own.

E - Engaging yourself in the world around you, viewing the world through the eyes of your inner child.

N - Networking, Networking, Networking—take every opportunity that comes your way to meet, greet and create relationships, not light and superficial relationships, ones that will enhance not only your life but also the lives of those you come in contact with.

T - Tenacity, being bold and stretching yourself beyond your current limits.

As we move forward into the glorious days ahead, take a look at the ground beneath your feet. See where you are standing today and ask yourself where you want to be standing tomorrow.

I would love to hear of your journeys! Happy Trails!

To Your Successes and Victories…

Innovation and Fun

Don't let the noise of other's opinions drown out your own inner voice. Most important—have the courage to follow your heart and intuition. They somehow already know what you truly want to become. Everything else is secondary.

~Steve Jobs

Happy Monday,

This past week I was again reminded of three truly great entrepreneurs of our time – Steve Jobs, Walt Disney and Yvon Chouinard. They have several things in common but the key qualities I found most relevant were:

- An incredible imagination and the ability to turn their visions into reality through innovation.

- A profound skill to make "work" play, not only for themselves but the people in their companies.

- Quality is job one, or as Yvon Chouinard simply puts it, in his company's mission statement, "Make the best product."

All three of these entrepreneurs have built companies and cultures that will (and in Walt's case have) surpass them long after they are gone from this planet. As I watched a video clip of Steve Jobs presenting the new iPhone at a recent Apple conference, his passion for what he does just oozed out of him. He really shared his pride for the individuals in the Apple organization that had made this incredible piece of new technology possible.

Watching this come from a man who did what it took to save Apple from the wrecking ball was inspirational. Steve took a $1 annual salary during lean times to save his company. In contrast, think about how other executives in major corporations take multimillion-dollar bonuses while they lay off thousands of workers. Or worse still, as our country faces trillions of dollars of debt, those in

Congress continue to give themselves pay raises. Steve Jobs has been a great example of how fiscal actions at the top trickle down to the health of the organization.

Yvon Chouinard is the founder of Patagonia and the author of the book, *Let My People Go Surfing*. It was my privilege to meet and get some hands on rock climbing techniques from Yvonne many years ago while working for a backpacking manufacturer in Southern California. He has created a culture and a product that has put smiles on people's faces (internally and externally) and his ideals have stood the test of time. I was impressed with him back then and continue to be as I see how he stuck to his beliefs and principles through all these years, in the good times and in the bad.

"Innovation" and "fun" while creating a quality product or service are the key words that seem to ring loudly through the stories of these three men and the companies they created. Innovation and fun – just the sound of them get my creative juices flowing in wanting also to create a company and be surrounded by companies that find these words in what they do everyday.

Was it always easy for these three? Heck no! Steve was fired from the very company he started only to come back and save it! Yvon was an avid outdoorsman trying to make a living doing what he loved. For Walt – can you imagine the pressure of going against the grain and buying swamp land for an amusement park or creating a little mouse named Mickey and convincing people of the idea! But just as his character Snow White and her little dwarf buddies sang, he believed in whistling while he worked. How many of us can share in that ultimate ability?

So as you move forward in your week ahead – where is the fun and innovation in your work? Does quality always come out as job #1 or does it get left out because of "not enough hours" in the day? How could you move your life towards doing more of what you love and less of what you "have" to do? What is stopping you? Who is stopping you? You could start right now, here today and begin giving back to the world some of the gifts you have received – simply by giving your full self to all that you do.

Wishing you a week of – innovation and fun! I know for myself as I continue down a path this week of creating a new business idea (more to come later!) the Entrepreneurial spirit of these three entrepreneurs will keep me whistling while I work!

To You Successes and Victories…

Vision Soaring

All victors are at first visionaries.

~Author Unknown

Happy Monday,

With the darkness outside my window this morning another week begins. It is interesting how we arise in the darkness many mornings knowing the light of day will come and take us where we need to go. The hope and vision of what will be…

Over the past week I had the opportunity, and as some say, the bringing on of good luck when on two different occasions a bald eagle flew overhead. A habit I picked up many years ago is always looking when a large bird flies overhead to see what kind of bird it happens to be, always hoping it will be an eagle. Many times it is a hawk (with a beauty all its own), sometimes a crow, occasionally a blue heron (beautiful with a prehistoric look to it) and rarely – very rarely – is it actually an eagle. In fact, I think it has been at least two or three years since I have seen one.

There is something regal and majestic about the eagle and the magnitude with which it flies and soars. Seeing the second one this week as it was soaring over the lake near our house, stopped me in my tracks. I enjoyed the few minutes it soared around the lake and watched until it became a distant little dot in the sky.

The vision of wanting the eagle to be there in the sky is almost as powerful as actually seeing one. Our visions and hopes are what indeed drive us to do what we do (or sadly don't do) with our lives. A few weeks ago in the Victory Circles we talked about visions for the year ahead and what we wanted to see happen to take us closer towards our definite chief aim. With a new calendar year unfolding, it is time to soar and make our visions realities. Keep your visions close to you… remembering to work towards them daily… and soar in between!

To Your Successes and Victories…

Eyes Wide Open

Vision is the art of seeing the invisible.

~Jonathan Swift

Happy Monday,

Well, here we are on the first Monday of springing forward and moving into Daylight Savings Time. Though we have to give up an hour this week I think it is so worth it with the signs of spring becoming more and more apparent each day. Yes, from the smell in the air to the longer days, and for those of us here in colder climates, that glorious green is starting to appear on the ground all around us.

The things we can visualize and see change from day to day… some, we plan and others just happen without any planning at all. This Saturday was a day of wonders for me as I experienced both of these types of events.

Saturday afternoon I marveled in the realization of several visualizations I have had over the past six months (and more) coming to fruition. One was a Zen garden I had visualized in a part of our yard that had become quite barren looking when we cut down a large dying bush last fall. Throughout the winter, thoughts and visions of this special meditation place came in and out of my head. I began looking for a unique Buddha statue to make this space really special. After many months of looking I found it, my special Buddha, and it all seemed to fall together. On Saturday, thanks to some creative and muscled work from Ed, our new Buddha, Guatama, found its new home.

The day before, on Friday, I experienced the coming together of a group of entrepreneurial women, the Victory Circle. Better even than my wildest dreams, this group of terrific women, several of whom I welcome to the Victory Letter this morning, have come together to assist each other along our way. I look forward to our monthly gatherings as we learn and grow from each other. (Authors Note: This letter was written the Monday after the very Victory Circle nearly five years ago!)

Now to the other side of the spectrum… and not seeing something coming towards you! Late Saturday afternoon as my daughter and I sat down to watch a movie, my body seemed to just break down on me. First, I couldn't breath very well. Then a horrible and I mean horrible pain began to develop in my abdomen. Trying to "deal" with it, I headed for the bathroom. As I lay there on the bathroom floor it became apparent that this was bigger than my sheer will would be able to make go away or could handle.

The next thing I knew I was headed towards the hospital laying down in the back seat of the car. All I could visualize at that moment was making the extreme pain go away. After a few Hail Mary's and an Our Father we arrived at the hospital. To make a painful story short, it turned out that I had bronchitis mixed with a urinary tract infection topped off by a passing of a kidney stone! Amazing things I never saw coming! The good news is that with a little medication and a few days rest I will be back at it!

As I lay in my bed yesterday afternoon looking out at my new Zen garden and the beautiful spring day, I was busy visualizing feeling better again! This all leaves me with no doubt in my mind that our vision whether in hindsight or foresight, can continue to assist us along our way. Most important, I guess, is that we remember to leave our eyes wide open for that which our mind and eyes cannot yet see.

Wishing you a week full of extra spring in your step!

To Your Successes and Victories…

Possibilities Abound

Faith is to believe what you do not see; the reward of this faith is to see what you believe.
~Saint Augustine

Happy Monday,

This Monday morning comes with spring gloriously everywhere outside my window! It is amazing how quickly the world around us is turning to my favorite color, green. We knew that spring would come and it did! Is it the power of belief or the power of being?

Saturday night we went out to celebrate our friend Lynette's birthday. After a delicious meal full of fun and good food we headed off to a local pool hall and played a little pool. It has been a while since I have played the game but as they say, it is like riding a bike and it comes back to you. What I was thinking as the little striped balls made their way into the holes – was, "Is it luck or indeed visioning and focus?" In my case, perhaps a little bit of them all three.

Our visions come to us step-by-step, piece-by-piece. Just like in the game of pool, you only win the game one ball at a time (sometimes two if you are very lucky). Yesterday, while looking around my garden and looking at the possibilities of what is to be in the months ahead, I knew the key was in remembering to take it on in baby steps.

For those of you who are new to the Victory Letter, I am an avid gardener with two acres of property. If I don't take it step-by-step it can quickly become very overwhelming this time of year. I also have learned to take it strategically because no matter how beautiful the weather may be right now, it is only March and Mother Nature has a mind of her own, and snow/frosts are possible into May. So for now I will visualize, plan and set my mind on what is to be in my garden as I begin the clean-up work from winter.

What are your visions and dreams in front of you right now, whether on a personal or business dimension? How much faith sits behind those visions? Do you believe enough in what you want to see happen to live each day bringing it to fruition? If it is a large vision, are you open to taking baby steps to get there? Whether you are setting off on a new marketing plan, a new product in your business or searching for a new path in your career – the key is to first create the vision, follow it with a strategic plan, and then of course have complete faith that it will work.

The power of nature will be unfolding before us in the weeks ahead with the trees budding into beautiful spring flowers and tulips emerging from the ground. Even the grass that sat brown and dormant each day looks a little greener. Let it be a continuous reminder of the possibilities all around us.

Wishing you the faith and belief to have your visions and dreams become a reality.

To You Successes and Victories…

Burning Desires

The starting point of all achievement is desire. Weak desires bring weak results, just as a small amount of fire makes a small amount of heat.

~Napoleon Hill

Happy Monday,

As the Monday morning sun begins its rise over the eastern plain, another week has begun. Thoughts of things to be done circulate in my head as I sip that delicious first cup of coffee. Outside my office window sits the statue of a pelican and it gets my attention this morning as I think about the interesting features of this bird whose desire for travel takes it thousands of miles every year.

I remember when I first gazed on a white pelican in Colorado and said, "Wait a minute what is that bird doing here?" They come to the little lake by our house each year and hang out for a while. They are beautiful creatures and I love to watch them fly and fish.

Just imagine if your burning desires in your life were so strong that they kept you focused enough to keep a strong momentum no matter what came across your path each day. Some days it can be tougher than others with e-mails, phone calls and other distractions left and right blocking your initial desire. Keeping to task and remaining focused can be the difference between success and failure in getting to where we ultimately want to go.

Of course, then comes the important part about enjoying the journey along the way.

So what are you focused on to achieve this week? What is your burning desire to see happen by this Friday, then the next Friday, and the next? What obstacles are in your way? How can you remove them? How strong is your desire, really? Is the journey enjoyable in between?

Close your eyes right now and imagine what it is you want to achieve. Who is it you wish to become or continue being? Every morning take a few minutes to open your mind once again to the desire burning inside you. Does something continue to block your way? What is it? How can you eliminate it from your life? Who is it that supports you in your quest for your desire? How can you have more of that kind of support around you?

While giving a talk last Friday, I met a man who really touched my heart when he came up to me afterwards and said through some tears, "You know, Victory to me is doing the cancer walk that my wife used to always do – I never did it because it was her thing. I lost her last year and now it is my turn to do it for her." He has found his burning desire, which is now helping him divert the passion he felt for his beloved wife.

Like Napoleon Hill says in the quote here in today's letter, a small fire does make a small amount of heat... what can you do right now today to get your flame burning brighter?

Wishing you a week full of focus and purpose!

To Your Successes and Victories...

True Potential

It is a wonderful truth that things we want most in life—a sense of purpose,
happiness and hope—are most easily attained by giving them to others.

~Isabelle Allende

Happy Monday,

Do you ever have those days when technology starts to overwhelm you? For me, crazy as it sounds, when I walk into my office during the early morning light (or lack thereof) I usually have about 18 little lights waiting for me from my printers, computers, telephone lines and surge protectors. Yes, my technology is waiting for me to take it by the hand and do what it needs to do in a given day.

I know that technology in its many forms is my friend, though some days, it just plain overwhelms me with its possibilities and yes, demands. With just a little scratching at the surface and looking past the "techno bumps," you can discover some incredible tools that are available to each of us. The possibilities of it all are amazing and a little overpowering at times.

Most days I would rather just not listen to those who speak of what is not possible but hear instead a visionary like Steve Jobs or Seth Godin talk about what is achievable. Not only what is probable, but for companies like Apple these days, consistently doable! Do you realize that on Christmas day alone they sold 20 million songs on iTunes? Quite true, in a "down" economy, they created $20 million in revenue electronically! And the best part is that they made people happy while doing it.

Attending several conference calls last week I was excited, delighted and yet overwhelmed (that "o" word again) at the possibilities of technology that I could add to my business. Just for a change of pace (yes, ok, I am a bit strange) I needed a calm in my technology overwhelm, so I used my computer to tune into Steve Jobs annual keynote address at the Apple Conference.

Just as I knew it would, listening to Steve took me away from my realm of "so much to do, so little time" and instead refreshed and renewed me with the latest and greatest new work toys from Apple. His ability to make complex programming sound fun, cool and, ah yes, that word we love to hear every business day – profitable – renewed my belief in overcoming the impossible.

There are people who would have you believe that there is nothing but gloom and doom in the world. The stock market is crashing; the recession is on the way – nothing good on the horizon. But just like with anything in our life – we just need to find the light in the storm, the place where you can find people giving back as easily as breathing.

Think about what you do every day in your work or play. When do you feel the most satisfaction? Is it when the work is humming along, allowing you to make things possible for not only yourself but for others? Is it when you build something from scratch or complete a project? Or perhaps when you see someone else complete something? When does the real true joy emerge for you? Can you, your company or organization make a profit doing this? Can the proverbial win/win be created?

Last week I created a new "blog", yes the "B" word. Truth is that it took me a couple of hours including the initial content. But at the end of the day I was able to see something new, take on a challenge and hopefully give something back to the world at large.

In your week ahead as you do what you do, what if you did it with complete passion, focusing on the process of giving. Opening up your heart, mind and spirit to believing in what it is that you have to give, closing out any naysayers in the process, and completely making your self-unhearing and oblivious to anyone who says you can't do something?

What you can accomplish in this single week ahead can make a difference not only in your life but also in the lives of those you touch by your work. Be that difference to your family, friends, coworkers, customers, and yes, people you don't even know. Imagine if you did it consistently week after week, year after year!

And no, you don't have to necessarily engage technology to make it possible (though it really can help).

Today is the day that we remember Martin Luther King, the man who based his life on giving, ultimately with his life. Wishing you the opportunities that abound when you believe that anything is possible, when you fully give what really is your true potential to give.

To Your Successes and Victories…

Giving Birth

Having a baby changes everything.

~Johnson & Johnson

Happy Monday,

As my fingers hit the keypad this morning the weatherman says it's a balmy three degrees outside. December has arrived! Brrrr, time to get warmed up inside, sip some nice warm coffee and to begin another week. When I heard this week's quote I had to laugh out loud as indeed having a baby does change everything...

From the very first moment that I read on the test strip that I was pregnant, so many things changed in my life. On the day my son made his arrival I felt emotions that I did not even know were possible to feel. I had given birth. Wow! It was love at first sight. Two years later I followed that up with my daughter and it was amazing how having just one more child made such a difference; we had created a family and I was truly in love with each member of it!

The truth is, the birth of my children has brought me great joy in my life and challenges me everyday to try and be a better person for them to call Mom. The challenges seem to get even stronger in their teenage years when they aren't as cute and cuddly. Daily now they challenge me in a much different way as they have more exposure to the world and little by little we have to let them begin to do things for themselves... a scary proposition.

But at the end of the day it is worth it, as the love I felt for my children at their birth still remains constant and strong. It gets me through the bumps and moments when they look at me as if I were an alien from another galaxy and they speak as if they are aliens from another planet.

If you think about it, giving birth to anything can change your world. It doesn't have to be a child; it can be a thought, an idea... a business venture. Just as parenting has its stages, so does birthing a business, and I have also birthed several of those along my way.

You have that early infancy stage when the high of your new business venture keeps you going through the sleepless nights when you are kept awake by a combination of excitement and fear. Then you progress into the toddler years when the business requires so much of your attention and is constantly on your mind. Slowly as your business begins to grow you can let go a bit and allow others to help you nurture it along. Then you get to the stage of the teenage years and it is telling you what to do!

The key is to be prepared as much as possible to handle anything and everything. Go with the ebbs and flows, learn from your mistakes and remember to be fully successful – giving up is not an option!

As you begin this week think about what you have given birth to in your lifetime. What have been the rewards? What has caused you stress or grief? What have been the changes that have occurred around you because you and you alone moved forward? Is it time to birth something again or to enhance what you have already created? Perhaps some extra nurturing is in order?

The great thing about the changes that occur with birth and rebirth are the possibilities this action creates. A new life unique unto itself is created! You will find that surrounding yourself with positive thoughts and inspiring people helps so much when that baby is crying or that teenager just said words to you that you would not have thought possible.

Ah yes, something that starts as a small idea or perhaps happens by accident, then turns into something more than you ever imagined… challenging your world and the world around you, hopefully bringing you fruits for your labor… and hopefully it is a labor of love. I wish you much prosperity and new life in the week ahead!

To Your Successes and Victories…

CHAPTER 2

Victory...
And Self-Confidence

The Law of Attraction as a Foundation to Grow Your Business and Life

Something for you,
Something for me,
That's the law of attraction
and self-confidence in simplicity.
Joyous and giving,
Listening and kind,
The gifts inside you are what you must find.

Perhaps the darkest time of my life, in which I held little to absolutely no self-confidence or esteem were the days of my teenage youth. Life was coming at me very fast. Many changes developed in my personal life that made it hard to even begin to know who I really was. It got so bad that at one point I simply saw no future—only today, and I didn't like what I saw. At the ripe young age of 15, one afternoon after a particularly horrible day of feeling like a misfit at a new high school, I decided enough was enough. With the words of "Ben" playing on my little stereo, I took an entire bottle of aspirin figuring that would do the trick.

I lay there on my bed looking for the relief that in those twisted moments I thought my life ending would bring. As the voice of Michael Jackson sang: "I used to say 'I' and 'me,' now it's 'us', now it's 'we'," over and over until it suddenly hit me that I needed to pull myself together and find the 'we' in my life again. After all, it completed the 'me' – especially at 15 years of age.

My mother had just remarried… I had new siblings… and we lived in a new town where I knew no one. I had left behind my very close girlfriends whom I had known my entire life. They had given me my self-confidence. They were a part of me – my "we."

In those moments, so many years ago, I lay there on my single bed, knowing that I indeed had to come to grips with what was going on in my head.

Suddenly I knew that I was in a situation where without fast action there would be no tomorrows to worry about. I yelled for my sister to help me, and thank God she did. She immediately called 911 and a stomach pump later I was back in action.

It was not an easy road rebuilding my self-confidence. Slowly but surely the years passed. I did the one thing anyone building self-confidence has to do, and that is to put one foot in front of the other each and every day. I found my way, carried on, and found the 'we' actually was right inside of 'me.'

Perhaps one of the biggest reasons for business failure I have seen, beyond the lack of cash flow is that the owner loses his or her self- confidence. Usually it is depleted by a single source: Fear.

Fear comes in many shapes and sizes but when it is not recognized or acknowledged for the power it can take from us, it can actually deplete our confidence to the point of immobility. Acknowledging doubt and fear and using it to pull us forward is indeed the first step to success and victory on so many levels. I like to ask myself when considering a new direction or venture, "What is the best possible thing that could happen if I moved forward with this idea or action?" I counter that question with, "What is the worst possible thing? And follow up with "What will happen if I don't do this at all?"

Money is usually the biggest culprit. The fear of not having enough can bring us to our knees and turn our world upside down. It can totally cause us to lose perspective and go running for the nearest employment opportunity – good, bad or indifferent. Many a promising business has been given up for the illusion of a "regular paycheck."

There is an old saying that goes, "If at first you don't succeed try, try again." A confident salesperson could have coined that phrase (but actually, it was an American school teacher). After all, isn't a successful sales person the ultimate tell all of confidence in ones self? She or he possesses the ability to take everything they believe in about their product or service and throw it out there for someone to say a big fat "no" to them.

The ability to master the art of persuasion (sales) and then combine it with the art of caring about the other person's true wants and needs is the sign of a really successful sales person on so many levels. That practice is sets one up for great success in business, and in life, especially for those who make it seem effortless. Here is where the law of attraction comes shining through.

We all encountered the salesperson who tried to cram their way of thinking into our head without showing any respect to us whatsoever. That person isn't really a sales person, rather more of a con artist trying to take advantage of us, someone who is only interested in taking something from us regardless of what value we actually receive. Similar to a spoiled child trying to get his or her own way, this kind of selling has no concern for the end result or overall effect on our side of the fence. Sadly, it is this type of sales person who creates a negative image of what a sales person in general.

In sales trainings I have conducted over the years I have requested that attendees who lack self-confidence, because of their fear of how others may "perceive" them, to try the following exercise. Draw a picture of your negative self-image as a sales person on a balloon. Then, with all your negative beliefs really focus on that balloon and go ahead, pop it! As you do, imagine all the air leaving the negative belief. Let that image help you to move forward leaving the bad image of you as a "salesperson" to dissipate into thin air.

Not too long ago, somewhere along my way, I heard the phrase, "sell belief" and it really rang true for me. I have always had the easiest of times selling ideas and things in my life that I had the strongest belief in. It's where the rubber meets the road, where everything just clicks into place and your business starts to hum. That is when you fully gain the trust and the right to call someone a customer or a client.

It makes me grin to think that I have spent the better part of my career in the field of sales… in one form or another. Quite a difference from that young teenage girl I used to be whose shyness and insecurities almost ended my life so prematurely. Finding strong relationships again in my life surely helped but so did the positions I came into in my career. In fact, a customer service position that almost overnight turned into a sales position became my turning point. This change in positions (or lose the job I had come to love) became an opportunity along my path that I have to now thank for turning my confidence all the way around.

Yep, there I was at the age of 21 traveling along without a clue as to where my "career" was headed. I randomly answered a classified ad for a company called Wilderness Experience. Thinking at first that it was an amusement park of some kind I was pleasantly surprised to find out that it was company that manufactured of all things, backpacks and other outdoor gear. Customer Service seemed pretty easy and I was delighted when I got the job, soon discovering I loved customer service and making people happy through problem solving.

Over the course of the first couple of years in that job I found that I was not only a competent person in business but also that customers liked and respected me. This was huge in building my ego and self-confidence.

Then the day came when the shift from customer service to sales came into play. My manager told us that we would have to assist our outside sales force as the company's bottom line had been slipping. Suddenly the comfortable job I loved became quite uncomfortable. But I worked my way through it and I will never forget the day I clinched a nearly half million-dollar sale. Quite a chunk of change for me, the novice city girl selling outdoor gear. It was most exciting because it happened by creating a win/win/win situation with the customer, the company and me.

What happened in order for that big sale to come about? I had spent a lot of time building a strong relationship with this client, having nothing more in mind than how I could be of service to their retail store. A "sale" became the natural outcome because I was able to have the customer see what I saw as a "must have" for his retail business. I had the belief that they would profit nicely from making the purchase. He in turn, saw and trusted in my belief.

With all of this in mind it is so important to remember that in one form or another each of us must be a sales person to get what we want out of life. And to sell what you have in order to gain what you want – with honesty and concern for others – takes self-confidence. The true success is in building a relationship with another human being that will stand the test of time, to share what we see in our mind's eye and to have others see it too, and have them "buy" what we have to "sell," as it comes in many ways, shapes and sizes. Again, you must believe in yourself as well as your idea, product or service.

In order to be an entrepreneur you must be a salesperson who has little to no self-doubt, because the moment you allow doubt to creep in, you begin to lose the game. It is amazing how much fear the tiny word "no" evokes, even sometimes in the most confident people. There are just two little letters in this small word, but they have been known to stop many people from asking for what they want, so fearful of the request being answered with a "no," so fearful of the "no" being a rejection of themselves.

The best way I have found to embrace the word "no" is to simply think of it as a way to open up a form of discussion. The most confident and successful veteran sales people realize that a "no" can actually be the beginning of a long-term relationship. A "no" can and usually does mean "not right now" or "not this particular product." It can even simply be possible that the prospective buyer does not have enough information or know you well enough to put that kind of trust in you. Again, I highly disagree with cramming it down someone's throat regardless if they want it or not. It is at this point that the fine skill of listening comes into play to help us really hear what is being said.

Another fear factor in the arena of sales is the dreaded "cold call." My opinion and strong belief is that your business should be set up in such a way that you should be able to rely on the contacts you have created along the way to generate new business. Sure, in your first couple of years of business you need to build your contact database but if after a few years you are still struggling with how to generate new business you are doing something wrong.

Creating relationships and continuous referrals in your business will give you a world of options when it comes to generating new business. It will also totally empower your self-confidence. The only way you should look at a cold call is as a way of getting to initially know a prospective client or colleague better. Patience is the name of the game and you should never ever use your initial contact with someone as a way to try to close a sale. That is unless the prospect is already eager to buy from you.

The law of attraction plays a big role. A sales person who is argumentative or combative will struggle with the art of persuasion. So focused on the need to be "right" or to have it their way, opportunities can be lost. Many great books have been written on the topic of sales and persuasion. But you can also find great inspirations in looking at the basics of human potential.

The words of St. Francis de Sales (How ironic though his name is pronounced sa-les actually is spelled s-a-l-e-s) can ring true when selling to others in your life whether a client, your boss, your spouse, or even your kids. St. Francis is credited with having said the words, "When you encounter difficulties and contradictions, do not try to break them, but bend them with gentleness and time."

St. Francis is also noted for saying the following words which act as a guiding light for those who don't give the sales process, along with the ability to belief in one's self, the time it requires: "Have patience with all things but chiefly have patience with yourself. Do not lose courage in considering your own imperfections but instantly set about remedying them – every day begin the task anew."

Enjoy the Victory Letters of this chapter as they pertain to the beautiful gift we give to ourselves when we build our own strong and unique form of self-esteem while embracing the *Master Mind Principle of Self Confidence*.

Shining Star

All riches, of whatever nature, begin with a state of mind.

~Napoleon Hill

Happy Monday,

As I look out my window I see the morning star shining brightly as night turns into day. There is a belief that if you wish on the only star in the sky your dreams will come true… *believing*, I think, can make it happen. Another key in making your dreams come true is confidence. Yes, indeed the confidence to move forward.

Napoleon Hill continues the above quote in his book, ***The Master Key to Riches***, "and let us remember that a state of mind is the one only thing over which any person has complete, unchallenged right of control." I don't know about you but as a child and teenager I was very shy, almost to the point of stopping me from getting anything done in my life. It used to make my stomach hurt. Being in a social situation (ugh) was the worst.

That was until I started building my confidence. In thinking about how it happened, the truth is I just went out and made myself do things – you know, I took myself out of my comfort zone to try to get where I wanted and needed to go. There are still times today that I must give myself a big push but it seems after a little while of doing something that I have not done before, it gets easier. Confidence gets built.

In the book mentioned above, Napoleon Hill lists the 12 riches in life and I think each of them applies to building confidence:

1. A positive mental attitude.

2. Sound physical health.

3. Harmony in human relationships.

4. Freedom from fears.

5. The hope of achievement.

6. The capacity for faith.

7. Willingness to share one's blessings.

8. A labor of love.

9. An open mind on all subjects.

10. Self discipline.

11. The capacity to understand people.

12. Economic security.

So as you move forward in your week ahead I wish your star to shine brightly. With that, I wish you the confidence and grace to share with the world all the gifts you have to offer.

To Your Successes and Victories…

Cutting the Waves

It's not the size of the ship that makes the man seasick…
it's the motion of the ocean.

~Unknown

Happy Monday,

Well here we are again… with another Super Bowl Sunday come and gone. To our friends and family in PA congratulations on your win! This morning I find myself moving a bit slow and dealing with a couple of sick kids, as the cruds seem to have moved into our house.

With teenagers it seems easier to deal with bad colds by making them soup and tea than it is to fix all the other things that ail them. Saturday night we attended the 50th Birthday party of my good friend Debbie. Written on her community poster birthday card was today's quote. How appropriate it seems in a world that gets us a bit seasick at times, especially for our young people who have so much to digest from the ocean all around them.

Perhaps my favorite part of the Super Bowl yesterday was the Dove commercial that addressed the importance of improving self-esteem in young girls. I was impressed that Dove took the time and money to deal with an issue that is so important. Self-esteem is probably one of the greatest gifts we can give our kids and ourselves for that matter.

How many times in your life have you been slowed down or even stopped in moving forward because you doubted yourself? Or maybe you lacked the courage to move forward on something important in your life because you did not believe enough in yourself? It has happened to us all and it can be a very lonely place indeed. I think the greatest gift we can give our kids (and ourselves!) is the belief in their own ability to be and do all that they can.

In the week ahead… let's look around us and help someone in our lives by acknowledging their strengths and by showing our gratitude to them directly for what they add to our lives? Sometimes it can be as simple as just really listening to what someone has to say and helping to make the ocean a little less choppy as we all carry on together in our journey.

Wishing you a great voyage in the week ahead!

To Your Successes and Victories…

Dive Deep

Be not the slave of your own past—plunge into the sublime seas, dive deep,
and swim far, so you shall come with self-respect, with new power,
with an advanced experience, that shall explain and overlook the old.

~Ralph Waldo Emerson

Happy Monday,

Upon reading this quote I envisioned diving into a pool, feeling the water surround me and moving forward to the other side. Luckily, I was sitting by a pool at the time and went right for the diving board and did just that. How great it was to feel the water surround me as I entered the world that was waiting for me underneath. Whatever direction I chose to go was possible… it was all up to me.

Isn't that a great thought… to just escape sometimes? To go ahead and leave those preconceived notions that we let block our minds and swim towards the other side. How many times do we let thoughts stop us from being all we want or can be in this lifetime? Think about when you are swimming and it just happens because you let your body pull you forward.

Driving back from California I watched with amusement and delight as my daughter, Bailey, decided to pass the time by waving to drivers as we passed them. Her theory was that they were either "sweet" or "sour" depending on their reaction or lack of reaction to her. The truckers got an additional request as she made the motion with her arm for them to honk their loud horns.

At first I went about my driving not paying much attention to what she was doing but as the hours wore on, she didn't stop or tire of this game. I found myself becoming interested and amused at the reactions of people and even more so in her continued playing of the game. After many rejections from truckers to honk their horns she got three in a row to honk. We both began yipping it up to the point that Travis in the back of the van wanted to know what was going on. Next thing I knew he too was involved wanting to get others' reactions. They did it for most of the two-day drive home to Colorado.

I think what stood out for me the most is that they did not let the rejections get to them. They kept going, keeping in mind only the fun of when someone responded to them. What a great way to think about looking toward the future by remembering the good outcomes in our life and not focusing on the bad, remembering the smiles and not the frowns. It goes back to Sales 101... keep your mind on the yes's and not the no's.

So as you plunge into a new week, keep your mind fresh to the possibilities in front of you. Keep the words of Mr. Emerson in front of you to remembering to dive deep if you must and to make your swim in this life refreshing and challenging. Happy diving!

To Your Successes and Victories...

Signs of Spring

When you change the way you look at things, the things you look at change.

~Wayne Dyer

Happy Monday,

Spring began springing this past weekend with glorious blue skies and 60 degree days here along the front range of Colorado. The Rocky Mountains up above our foothills were covered in beautiful white snow and they looked magnificent against the blue of the sky. Those of you who made it to the slopes, I can only imagine what great skiing it was for you.

Ah spring, I so do love this time of year as we once again watch Mother Nature do her magic and change the landscape all around us. I was pleasantly surprised yesterday when I went to play a little in my garden (I just couldn't resist any longer) and found the soil ready to be turned; to my delight, a pansy was smiling at me from my pansy bed. The little signs of new growth were all around, including the grass that is starting to leave its winter brown behind and beginning the turn to that beautiful green.

Yes, of course it means new chores and responsibilities but they are chores and responsibilities that really do bring peace to my soul. I read a question a couple of days ago that I have been mulling over in my brain. The question was, what were the top ten, top moments of confidence I have had in my life? Wow, what a question to think about and ponder. You know, some were easy to identify, like the day of my marriage and the days that my children were born. But as for the rest of my monumental moments of self-confidence I had to really stop and think about what they were and what made them so special.

What I realized after writing down each of the ten things, was that the majority of those moments of confidence were surrounded by a change in my life of some kind. Situations like moving from one stage of life into another, from one season to the next. One was the day I graduated from grade school. Since I went to my grade school for eight years it was a very big deal, especially because I was leaving Catholic school and going into a public school in my ninth grade year. But I was extremely excited and confident as I went forward towards that new challenge.

What I also now realize is that the confidence was usually preceded by fear. Yeah, as I write this I realize that fear is there for sure when these moments of big change happen. Fear does seem to be a major predecessor to confidence. Hmmm, very interesting, it really is using fear wisely that makes us most confident.

For instance, the moments I delivered each of my two children, I wondered if I could handle the pain. Would it be a long delivery? And of course most scary of all… would I be a good mother? But as the seasons change and leave us no choice but to go with them, I was committed to becoming a mother. There was no turning back – it was going to happen. The moments that both Travis and Bailey were born I knew that all was right with the world and my confidence along with my mothering instincts kicked in just as they should have. Yes, it all seems to be part of the great plan.

So this week as you notice the signs of spring starting to appear all around you, think about those moments of great confidence in your life. Think of the new beginnings that happen with change and how they make our life more joyous… even if it is a bit scary along the way. Change is good when we let it happen as it should. And perhaps the next time you feel fear… get excited because confidence is just around the corner.

Wishing you a week full of confidence and blue-sky days!

To Your Successes and Victories…

Sharing Ideas

A desire accomplished is sweet for the soul.

~Proverb

Happy Monday,

On Saturday I hosted a yearly sales retreat. This is the third year running I have put on this event. It has been a great way to start off the year as we look at our possibilities for the 365 days ahead of us.

As two weeks of this new year have quickly come and gone, doing all we can to clarify as well as sustain our hopes and plans for the year ahead is vital. I have heard people say that New Year's resolutions don't work and, to the contrary, I think they do work if you set intentions and strong desires behind them. Add a strong plan of action and you are setting yourself up for success.

One of the things we discussed on Saturday is that being in the field of sales can be a challenge that pushes every emotional button inside of us. As a sales person you put yourself out there risking rejection and failure on a constant basis. But looking beyond that negative, the truth is that the rewards are many. Here are just a few:

- Building many great relationships.

- Helping others find new products and services that improve their lives.

- Open-ended income potential.

- The ability to learn and grow.

- Discovering new possibilities within yourself.

And perhaps the greatest thing I have found is the ability to visualize something and watch it come to life.

In truth, we are all sales people with ideas, various wants, needs and desires that once implemented will give happiness in various shapes and forms. By having those who make a difference in our lives understand and embrace our thoughts and dreams, we are just one step away from optimum happiness – aren't we? Are you ready to unleash your sales person within? Are you ready to let go of stereotypes you may have in your head about sales people and perhaps even have someone else's ideas make a difference in your world? Are you ready to have the best year possible?

Wishing you a great week ahead filled with possibilities and ideas to share!

To You Successes and Victories...

Facing Fear

Whatever you fear most has no power—it is your fear that has the power.

~Oprah Winfrey

Happy Monday,

…And a Happy Halloween! As I look out my window this morning with the fog thick as can be it seems that it is an appropriate setting for Hollows Eve. With this day being one of ghosts, goblins, monsters and things that go bump in the night it seems that fear would be the key word to talk about in today's Victory Letter.

Do you remember the first time you felt fear and fright? I'll never forget my first Frankenstein movie and then how Frank managed to accompany my dreams for a long time after. You know, that waking up in terror feeling that he indeed was coming after me and me alone. I would lay there in my bed afraid to move for what seemed like hours on end. But as the years came and went my fear of those nighttime creatures seemed to subside and finally disappeared altogether.

I do remember going on scary roller coaster rides, and the best way to deal with the fear was to close my eyes. Closing my eyes allowed me to keep the fear subsided (a bit anyway), make it through and conquer the ride. The funny thing is that friends, and even Ed for that matter, thrive on the thrill of a roller coaster… I guess one person's fear can indeed be another one's thrill.

The reality of it is we each have our own threshold of fear… our own individual fear factor. What is yours? There are many things that come into our life… let's see what could cause fear…

1. A job interview/new client interview

2. Dealing with an unreasonable boss (go back to item 1)

3. Not having enough month at the end of the money

4. Starting a new business

5. Watching our kids go out on their own

6. Giving a presentation in front of people

7. A big mean-looking dog

8. Your car breaking down on a dark lonely road... at night

9. Hiking in the middle of a lightening storm

10. A snake crossing our path

11. A big ugly-looking spider

12. Turbulence on an airplane (it gets me every time)

13. Change

I will stop at lucky 13, but how easy was it for me to come up with those in just a few minutes. The truth is that we could easily let our fears take over, stop us from doing many things in our lives, and make us miserable. Or we can let our strength guide us straight through the fear on to something much better.

Many of the great leaders of our time have made statements about the fears they have felt, from Oprah Winfrey in this letters quote to Mark Twain. Twain said, "Courage is resistance to fear, mastery of fear – not absence of fear." Sometimes, like on the roller coaster, it is easier to close your eyes and go for the ride and other times indeed we do have to face it straight on.

Many performers say that the fear they experience before going on stage actually makes them better at their craft (I think this is true in sales also). The strength and adrenaline that it gives them allows them to get on the stage and be the best they can be.

Hope your day today, as well as the week ahead, has only a few frights, very few tricks, and many, many treats.

To Your Success and Victories...

The Power of Attraction

You can light a fire on top of your place of business and people will notice you.
Or you can light a fire in your heart and people will come to you.

~Joe Vitale

Happy Monday,

I recently took on the challenge of registering for a course on how to get the perfect customer. Now, "perfect" is not a word I usually use – being that we live in a pretty "imperfect" world. But I liked the sound of the course since it was based on the law of attraction, a great instinctual principle to get in step with, so I went for it.

The bi-weekly teleclasses started this past week and I am excited about the possibilities before me over the next three months of the class! I have discovered that I am a life-long student of causes and effects, how what we do and how we think can make our lives brighter and richer.

I first heard about the power of attraction as way of thinking quite a few years back when I was taking my formal "coach" training. Ironically, at the same time we had just gotten our precious Labrador, Samantha. She was a living, breathing, white, fur ball of attraction and a great way for me to fully engage in the concept. Taking her everywhere I went, every single person that she and I came in contact with became like soft butter in her presence. People who normally might have never said even a word to me were talking up a storm.

Of course I thought, "Wow there is something to this power of attraction thing!" Samantha's cute, cuddly innocence was irresistible and I loved just watching the power she had over people! Now at nearly eight years old, there is still an essence about our Sammy that attracts people to her, but gone is that pure puppy energy that she once possessed. Now, she has to work just a little harder to attract people – but not much!

How is your attraction radar working for you these days? Do people come to you or run from you? I have found that there is a confidence that comes with attraction (a puppy really doesn't care what people think), but more importantly as Mr. Vitale shares in this week's quote it is that warmth in our hearts (as well as the puppy's) that starts to get contagious. Ever notice how a puppy will just run up and lick you for no apparent reason at all – except maybe that it is spilling over with love and excitement about life?

When someone is excited about something new in their life or a new business venture or product, etc. there can be no stopping them in sharing that excitement.

What is your excitement?

What sets your heart on fire?

What is it you love to think about, act on and do?

Do you try and incorporate it into your daily life and business?

If not, what if you did? If you do, what if you did it even more?

In this month of love – what if you shared what it is you love with those around you? What would come back to you? What would you attract into your life? What would come into the life of those you shared it with?

As we count down to Valentine's Day next week – don't forget about what warms your heart, because when you do you can't help sharing the love!

Wishing you the warmth and attraction that comes into your life in the week ahead as you spend time loving what it is you do!

To You Successes and Victories…

Blue Skies

No one can make you feel inferior without your consent.

~Eleanor Roosevelt

Happy Monday,

As the engines begin their weekly roar, the sun rises in the sky and it's time to get out there to live another week of our lives. What is on your agenda for the week ahead? How are you feeling from the inside out?

Your performance on any given day is dependent on just how much you, embrace yourself, giving you that old "Atta girl (or boy)", and appreciate all it is that you bring into your own life, from the love you feel for your family and friends to the contributions you make in your work. Take a look at what was the best thing you did last week. What did you do to either to make yourself better in one way or another or to assist someone around you?

In my Victory Circle last week we discussed the power of the Master Mind Principle of Self Confidence and what it means to us in our business and our lives. We talked about how combating our fears is the first step in bringing us closer to totally connecting with what we really have to give. Coming home from our gathering on Friday, I read today's quote from Eleanor Roosevelt and thought of the wonderful way she put it. We are indeed in control of how we feel about ourselves.

I know I am full of questions for you this morning but the next one has to do with what Eleanor had to say. Is there someone or something that makes you feel less than you know you can be? You know, the minute they walk into the room the air just seems to suck right out of you? No matter how good a mood you might have been in – suddenly you are not. For whatever reason the way they interact with you just seems to consistently bring you down.

The first question to ask your self is why. Why do you allow them to do that to you? One thing I do know for sure is that we have the power in our life to choose how we allow others to treat us. It does not even have to be a person of authority

– it could be a colleague, a client, an employee or a subordinate, friend or family member that makes your day miserable just because of their poor attitude either towards the world or you in general (or so it seems).

Each of us has the opportunity and the right to surround ourselves with those who support and nourish us, and to fill our senses with people who give us the courage to face each new day or week with excitement and joy in our hearts. When we don't, we can find ourselves sporting a bad attitude as well.

I invite you in the week ahead to take a look at where you are supported in your life.

Who allows your self-confidence to truly soar?

Who is it that, whenever you are in their presence, gives you the courage to be at 100% positive capacity?

How can you arrange to spend more time with them and eliminate any time spent with those who don't support you?

The choice really is yours. If there is a will, there is always a way. Look towards your fears and what or who is fueling them. Find ways to reduce or perhaps even eliminate them all together. The power is within you to do so. You just have to want it badly enough.

I am wishing you a week full of positive possibilities. Yes, anything really is possible with the right mindset. In fact, it's funny, and I swear it's true – in the course of writing these final words I glanced outside. The clouds that previously filled the sky as the sun began to lighten the horizon have now broken away, making it a brilliantly blue-sky day outside my window! Makes me want to hum the Irving Berlin classic (with Willie Nelson singing along), "Blue skies, smiling at me – nothing but blue skies do I see!"

Bust through your clouds – who knows – you might even be able to make that grumpy person in your life smile! Have a great week ahead!

To Your Successes and Victories…

CHAPTER 3

Victory...
And the Habit
of Self-Control

Avenues to The Full Value
of Your Time and Money

Flowing thoughts bring mind

new places of discovery,

Creating new habits,

Learning the tools of the trade,

Being in control of what is

and where it is I am going

47

The ability to write is perhaps one of the first gifts we are given where we see what happens in short order when we take it on as a new discipline. Do you remember the first time you took a line and turned it into a letter and you wrote for the very first time? The lined paper, the trying, the tongue pressed between the lips as you gave it your all? You're A's turning to B's and C's all the way to Z… just like the alphabet that circled the upper walls of your classroom?

At first it seems nearly impossible, but then, after much concentrated effort and control, you could write. I first learned the art of writing when I was somewhere between 5 and 6 years old. With a big brother and sister already fine-tuned at making letters into words I was determined to do it also (as I was with most things they were already doing). The first time I spelled out C-H-E-R-I on a piece of paper and realized that it created my own name, and it thrilled me! This single major victory embedded itself into my brain.

As time wore on I began to love to read and dreamed of one day becoming a world-renowned author. My problem along the way was not caring too much for school, getting bored with the day-to-day grind and subjects that did not interest me. I was also perhaps a little frightened by "proper" English. I let the dream slip away until my late 20s when enrolled in some classes at the local university here in Boulder, Colorado. Once again I became very intimidated by what I wanted to achieve.

Then I met two women who showed me the light and mentored me in the practice of letting my ideas and thoughts actually flow onto paper. They taught me the self-control of letting not just any formed words come onto paper but *my* words, *my* thoughts. The key was to forget, for the time being anyway, whether or not the words were structured properly. It was a true awakening. For me, self-control in writing came from letting my authentic self emerge.

One of the ladies who mentored me towards my writing self was Ying Chang Compestine, a writer herself who taught a few classes at the university. It was her real world successes and ideas that sparked me into believing that I could do it, that yes, I could become a writer.

The second woman was Cynthia Morris, a writing coach, who held regular free writing sessions in her home here in Boulder. I found myself instantly connecting to this form of writing – just letting the millions of words that form regularly in my head and allowing them to collect on paper. The key for me was hushing my inner English Critic and not allowing any feedback during this process. Words good, bad or indifferent were just allowed to flow and flow, and flow some more.

I really began to look forward to the weekly "free write" gatherings. Even as I write these words today, recalling the memories of those moments in Cynthia's tiny apartment, I get a warm and fuzzy feeling inside. With just a handful of people in her cozy little apartment in Boulder, Cynthia would give us a random topic to write about and without any other prompts we were set free to just let the words flow. And remarkably, flow they did.

Perhaps the most compelling part about the free writes was how one general topic would lead to six or seven (the number of people in the room) entirely different stories or theories on the same topic. It was intriguing, inspiring and simply great learning, mixed with fun. Believe me, when fun is added to learning it is highly effective.

It was during these free writes that I first created the concept for the Victory Letters, a way to speak from my heart and soul about the happenings in life around me. What I noted in these writings was that victories are possible for each of us every day, if we take the time to notice. What so intrigued me when I later started writing the Victory Letters and actually sending them out via e-mail, was how great they made me feel when I hit the "send" button. A new discipline in self-control was created as I made a vow to start each week, writing about something positive.

Yes, right out of the hopper every Monday morning I was able to creatively create!

While exciting and gratifying to hit that "send" button every Monday morning, the fact that the people receiving my positive thoughts were colleagues, clients, friends and family members (usually our biggest critics) made it even more thrilling. There was something about "putting it out there" that made it seem more real. My readers in fact without knowing it became my accountability partners – insuring that I would write every Monday morning come rain or shine.

An amazing thing began to happen… I started getting the most positive responses not only from those I knew very well but also from people I barely knew at all. It filled my heart and creative spirit more than I can tell you. The truth is it is one thing to write and another to have people share with you that what you have written made a difference in their life. That perhaps more than anything has inspired me to keep writing.

The next step was to reach my ultimate goal of actually writing a book. My office is filled with a multitude of books and I was always amazed by the many more multitudes that Cynthia had in her tiny little apartment! She had one entire wall of her apartment filled with book after book after book. When one floor to ceiling bookshelf would get full she would just get another one.

During our free writes I would look at these books and wonder if I might have one sitting on the shelf one day? It became a burning desire inside my soul, a desire that was accomplished when I did in fact write my first book, *The Victory Letters – Inspiration for the Human Race*. I proudly gave the book to Cynthia – to put on her shelf.

An unexpected benefit to writing, one that I hadn't anticipated ten years ago when I started to think of myself as a "writer," is the credibility that my words would bring to my business life. Really, I can't begin to stress this enough. In this day of so much written information being transmitted via emails, blogs and web content it is an important extra tool in your toolbox that you should not be without.

Writing is a channel for you to express yourself and have the world hear you. What does it take to make it happen? Again the answer is that essential element of self-control and making yourself do something. As our many teachers over the years have told us, practice makes perfect. While perfection is always hard to come by, opening your mind to the exercise and resulting possibilities is what Victory is really all about.

For many the excuse not to write is all wrapped up in the simple element of time. I shall never forget my mom's final days on the planet a little over a year ago when she knew that her end was imminent – in only days or weeks. It was there in the hospital that she was finally ready to put her memories down on paper with me as the transcriber. Sadly, with an extremely full 80 years to talk about, we barely got past high school.

How many things in your life have you put off getting done because of the excuse of no time? The proverbial "tomorrow" has been the thief of many a dream. Perhaps our most precious commodity is our time. Time is money, they say, and as a woman entrepreneur I know that to be true. The roles and responsibilities we have in our businesses and our personal lives can be overwhelming.

Managing time, or as I like to think of it – honoring time, is like taming a wild horse; no matter how much you try to control it, the control piece will not happen unless you feel extreme confidence while working with the minutes of each day. There are a variety of tools that we can incorporate along the way to get the most out of our time. It is such an important element to our success that, as noted in the introduction to this book, I created a Master Mind Principle around this key component

Years ago I took an intensive coach training workshop from the success coach and writer, Jennifer White. Her first book, **Work Less, Make More**, was about how she had learned to enjoy her work and her life by making the most important details a priority.

The ironic and sad life lesson that I got most from Jennifer, a bright and enthusiastic lover of life, was just how precious and fragile life is for each of us. Only a few months after I took the training her life was tragically cut short. She was about 30 years old and developed a brain aneurism during an international flight and died. Brilliantly, she had shared with the world several books, a syndicated column and her training programs. Just imagine that if she had not completed all that work, waiting for a tomorrow that was never to come. Myself, and so many others wouldn't have benefited from her knowledge, her generous desire to share her successes – or even know her name.

The bottom line that I will say one more time is this; the time we have this very minute is all we are assured of in this life. By putting off until tomorrow what we need to do today, even if it is just to stop and smell the flowers, could be a critical mistake. Our time is always of the essence so we need to spend it wisely, gaining the habit of self-control around it.

Along those same lines, we must also create habits and self-control around the element of money. This single resource can be the single driving force that either brings us great joy or great pain. The key, and a Master Mind Principle worth learning more about is that money as they say, makes the world go round.

Napoleon Hill in his epic classic, *Think and Grow Rich*, a must-read that I was given in my twenties, held as one of its major messages, the importance of the habit of saving money. Mr. Hill had this to say on the topic, "Anybody can wish for riches, and most do, but only a few know that a definite plan, plus a burning desire for wealth, are the only dependable means of accumulating wealth." *Think and Grow Rich,* was first published in 1937 during a time when the United States was still recovering from its first major economic downturn of modern times due to the Stock Market Crash of 1929.

In his book, Mr. Hill had this to say, "Poverty and riches often change places. The 1929 Crash taught the world this truth, although the world will not long remember the lesson. Poverty may, and generally does, unexpectedly take the place of riches. When riches take the place of poverty, the change is usually brought about through well-conceived and carefully executed PLANS. Poverty needs no plans. It needs no one to aid it, because it is bold and ruthless. Riches are shy and timid. They have to be 'attracted'."

Perhaps, the best way to then sum up the element of creating a habit around something is have a carefully orchestrated plan. Planning for your financial success, which includes saving money is crucial. Put into practice, the proverbial, "Saving for a rainy day." And as we have experienced in our own economic crash of this century – undoubtedly they come in one form or another.

Money, just like time, requires that you find a method of having enough stashed away – especially when those unexpected events in life happen leaving you really needing some "extra" money. Habitual saving is a key component to your Victory in this area – otherwise you just won't have the critical nest egg when it is most needed. Saving money is a trial and effort proposition. See what it will take for you to easily and happily put 10-20% of your income away in a secure place – making it a regular and consistent habit of which you have total self-control.

Barbara Hall, in her novel, *A Summons to New Orleans*, had these words to say:

"Because you are in control of your life, don't ever forget that. You are what you are because of the conscious and subconscious choices you have made."

As you move into these letters on the topic of self-control – think about how you spend your money and much more precious and harder to regain – your time. Ask yourself how in fact you are going to master the ***Master Mind Principle of Honoring Time*** and the ***Master Mind Principle of Creating a Habit to Save Money.***

Priming Your Pump

A mind stretched by a new idea, never regains its original dimensions.

~Oliver Wendell Holmes

Happy Monday,

There are times and moments in your life that are precious and unforgettable. At the moment that they happen you may not even realize how they will stay with you all the days of your life.

Over the past five days, I spent time in L.A. with my mom, helping her with a variety of things. One of them was going through a large pile of old family pictures. Many made me smile as I looked at pictures of myself as a child along with my brother and sisters. Some made me a bit sad, remembering people like my father, grandparents, aunts and uncles whom I will never see again.

One picture though, took my breath away and I thought I would share it with you here this morning. (Authors Note: This picture is actually the lead picture of this chapter.) Out of the piles of pictures it emerged, gloriously and so unexpectedly. It was a picture of the water pump that was located right outside the kitchen door of my grandparent's farm in Missouri. The photo was taken in the summer of 1964.

Over the years I have held a memory of my grandfather showing me how to use the pump that summer, the summer I turned 7 years old. The pump was used to give water to the farm animals. He showed me in his comical way (he always made me laugh) how the water would not just come from one swing of the pump but that I had to prime it first. It took me almost our whole stay there to finally get the water to come out. Either I gave up too early on most tries or my little arms wore out. I felt so proud when I finally got it to work (with quite a bit of help from my Grandpa).

What was so unusual about finding this picture was that there was no one in the picture, just the pump by itself. It made me stop and wonder who took the picture, knowing the importance of the pump, and giving me such a wonderful gift so many years later. Most likely it was Mom.

Now I know I have talked about priming the pump in a Victory Letter or two over the years but seeing this wonderful picture brought to me such a profound sense of clarity. So with Easter having passed and thoughts of new life emerging with the arrival of spring, finding the picture of this glorious pump – well it just cries for words about pump priming!

The priming that I speak of is our internal priming that we must do to be all that we can be, to enjoy life to the fullest. The priming can be for our creative juices, for restoring our wellness, health and well-being or even for our spiritual nature.

Whatever your belief of the greater spirit that carries your heart and soul, it needs to be nurtured. Last week I shared with you the fact that I am a recovering Catholic. While I say that "tongue in check," it has taken many years for me to be comfortable with my spirituality in the form I may need on any given day.

I don't go to church all the time but when I do go, I do so with an open heart and mind. Last Friday while in L.A. taking my mom to the doctor's office and running errands she asked if I would mind stopping by her church so she could say a prayer in honor of Good Friday. Of course I did not mind. In fact, given a choice to go to church with anyone, my mom is always my favorite church companion. Her deep belief and the depth of her prayer while she is in church always fill my heart and my soul.

It was a surprise to us that when we got into the church it was full of people waiting for something. In a few minutes we discovered that it was the 8th grade class of the church's school giving their rendition of the Stations of the Cross. It included a student portraying Jesus and carrying the cross. Many aspects of it touched my heart, even to the point of tears. What I realized as Mom and I emerged from the church after the service was that my spiritual pump had just been primed. Being there with Mom, especially after the roller coaster of her health this past year and a half, I felt incredibly blessed by the power from beyond.

So my question for you this week is how are you priming your pump?

What part of your heart, mind, body or soul do you feel needs a little extra attention?

What will it take to allow you to fully pull what you need from your ever-abundant well?

What or who are the persons, places or things in your life that keep you in tune with your inner core, your inner well?

Where is that place that allows you to feel the gratitude and the blessings of your life?

In the week ahead I wish you thankfulness as you reap the benefits of that which you sow. May there be many blessings flowing ahead for you!

To Your Successes and Victories…

Improving Habits

We are what we repeatedly do. Excellence then is not an act, but a habit.

~Aristotle

Happy Monday,

This morning as I sit here drinking my coffee thinking about these words of Aristotle and the week ahead, I ponder over the thought of excellence and the power of good habits vs. bad habits or even what it takes to acquire a habit at all.

When I was in my early 20s and had moved to Colorado I was faced with eliminating a habit I had picked up in my teens. It took me a couple of years to want it really badly enough but I finally did it… I quit smoking. Not an easy task whatsoever, but today the smell of cigarette smoke gags me. A bad habit was turned into a good one, and it was probably one of the hardest habits I ever had to change as well as one of the best things I ever did for myself.

The truth is, every day we are faced with improving ourselves and trying to achieve excellence or some facsimile of it… no easy task. In the 80s I was fascinated when Tom Peters came out with his book, *In Search of Excellence*.

Since the day I started my first company, I really did want it to be the best, to give my customers the best and have my employees be their best. It was not always an easy task especially when I tried to balance it with profitability, but when I achieved certain goals I found my customers were delighted and it fueled me to continue. It became the foundation for my business philosophy… and yes, a habit.

Does it mean perfection? I don't think so, more than perfection, it is simply doing the best you can – depending on what you have to work with in your life on any given day. Otherwise, you can make yourself crazy and thoroughly stressed out. The key is finding the balance between *what's reasonable* and making excuses for not doing your best.

What are the habits in your life that you have achieved excellence in? What are the habits you would like to acquire? One for me has been making exercise a part of my daily life. No easy feat for me, while finding myself usually too busy with all the roles I play in my life. But the truth is, I know it's good for me and that not only does it help me to look better but to feel better too! So onward I go in my life to make this a habit.

They say (yes, those people who are out there saying things) that it takes 21 days to make an action a habit, something you start to do unconsciously without really even thinking about it. What is a new habit that you want to acquire… that if you started today you could be doing easily and effortlessly 21 days from now… something that could be embedded into your life?

We really do have so many opportunities before us in our lives… all we have to do is make the decision to go for it! I wish you a great week ahead as you savor all your possibilities and all that you can indeed achieve!

To Your Successes and Victories…

Simplistic Complexities

Happiness is not a matter of intensity but of balance and order
and rhythm and harmony.

~Thomas Merton

Happy Monday,

I awoke early yesterday and with my eyes half open saw the most beautiful "moon set" outside my bathroom window with the pinks of the morning sky first catching my attention. I headed into the kitchen to make the morning pot of coffee. Out of the kitchen window I saw the beauty of the moon getting ready to set over our beautiful Rocky Mountains to the west. The pinks and blues of the sky contrasted with the white of the moon and snow-capped peaks. It was a sight that I just wanted to hold on to and never let go.

Of course that would constitute holding on to time – something we cannot do. I knew in a moment or two the full moon would quickly be setting behind the mountains and there was absolutely nothing I could do about it. It was just the message I needed, as only two mornings earlier I seemed to have hit a proverbial wall worrying about deadlines. I had worked for nearly three straight weeks in a row and was rapidly reaching burnout. Through it all I knew I had my taxes to get finished over the weekend and there would be little time for fun.

Time is a funny thing – we use the phrase "time management" – when indeed we can't really manage time. For the most part it can end up managing us unless we find balance in our life. Balance between work and play – what we do and don't want to do with the time we are given – is pretty critical. How many times in the past week have you heard yourself or someone else say those words that come so easily to our lips, "I'd love to but I don't have enough time"?

So I spent a great deal of the day yesterday reflecting on time and the role it currently plays in my life. I pondered on how I could have more time to actually stop to smell the roses or for that matter even see the roses, as I searched for what is most important to me. In the process, I realized that in my excitement to get this new year off to a great start, many of the seeds I had sown had all started growing at once. My knee jerk reflex was to just add more hours and days to my work week.

Now, taking a deep breath I have decided to stop and take a look at what creates my rhythm and harmony while in the process finding it in myself to start having more fun again! All work and no play can make me a dull and not so happy girl. Did you notice that I am not looking to find more time – though it would be nice to open a drawer and find all this time just sitting in it!

However, this coming Sunday morning the majority of us here in the USA will each be given the gift of more daylight hours by daylight savings time going away until next Fall. The sun will stay with us longer each afternoon – at least giving us that illusion that we have more time in the day. To that I have one word to say – Hooray!

So as you move forward in the week ahead I invite you to look at how you spend your most precious commodity, your time. What drains you, what invigorates you, who and what giveth as well as who and what taketh away from you in your life. How often do you find yourself participating in the simple pleasures like laughing? As I focus on this simple yet complex issue in the month ahead I will share with you what I find!

Wishing you a little hickory dickory dock as you find ways to jump over the clock!

To You Successes and Victories…

Life Happens

It's a bad plan that admits no modification.

~Publilius Syrus

Happy Monday,

Today's letter is coming at bit late as I am writing to you from Steamboat Springs. And truth be told, I am running slower than normal as I sit here by the fire writing to you this morning. Then of course, I will have to go find an Internet connection to send this to you… somehow you will have this before the end of the day. One of the great things about taking a few days off is that sometimes the best plan is to have no plan at all, to just go with the flow. I may ski, hot tub and then send this… who knows for sure.

Last Friday morning while running around trying to meet several deadlines, preparing for a teleconference, and preparing to leave town for this family trip to Steamboat, I looked up from my desk and got stopped in my tracks. Out my office window I observed a scene provided by Mother Nature that was something out of an Ansel Adams picture. It was quiet surreal. There was frost on the bare trees and a little dusting of snow from the night before. The sun was just thinly seeable through the cloud cover and almost looked like the moon. It was perfectly framed by the trees in front of me. It was breathtaking.

Now, I was busy and had no time to stop to look at this incredible sight. Then the reality hit me that this scene before me would be gone in moments. So I allowed myself to stop and reflect on this unique gift I had just been given, and sure enough as quickly as it came it was gone. Truth is, it was worth the time it took from me as it energized and excited me about what I was working towards… these beautiful days in Steamboat.

One of the greatest balance acts we must master in our lives is letting life happen sometimes without our schedule always dictating what a day may bring. If you are a planner you know the ups and downs of having a "to do" list in front of you. While they may all be things you want to do sometimes the pressure of getting them done is overwhelming and indeed is one of the reasons we live in such a stress-filled society.

What if we just let life happen? Had an overall game plan but didn't get totally freaked out if it didn't get done? Allowed our "to do's" to roll to a future place in time or found a better way, a "funner" way to get them done? You know what they say about the best-made plans. Sometimes they go astray, and is that really bad… or just life?

I know right now that sitting here clicking away on my laptop is where I am meant to be at this moment. By simply enjoying this and not getting stressed out about being "late," I find myself looking forward to the moments ahead. This will allow for the "work" that I must get done while on this trip to become my "play." That is one of the joys of being an entrepreneur; work can be play, as the time given for work and play blends together, allowing for the overall game plan to unfold as we go.

So as you move forward in the week ahead… what is your plan? Are you open to modification or is it so stringent that you will crack if it is not adhered to? On the other end of the spectrum, are your plans so loose that by the end of the week you will wonder what happened, not having accomplished anything?

Remember that the final accomplishment is what we make it… meeting a goal, having fun, spending time with someone, creating something, taking care of our physical needs, being and doing what we want and need. After all… isn't it our life?

So in the week ahead I wish you calm, peace and success… whatever that looks like for you!

To Your Successes and Victories…

Adventures in Creativity

We are all a part of the artwork, each one adds it's own splash of color.

~Linda L. Tessmer

Happy Monday,

The truth of the matter is indeed that every single one of us adds to the color of this world. I was reminded of this last weekend while having a truly wonderful time attending the festivities of Lisa's wedding, the daughter of one of my dearest and best friends, Linda Lou (as I fondly like to call her).

On the drive to the Pittsburgh airport, after 5 days of fun and festivities, Linda's words (this week's quote) reminded me of the reason I had enjoyed everyone's company so much. It was each person's particular color that made it so special. Had we all been the very same it could have been rather dull.

I will never forget watching Lisa walking down the aisle with Dave (her dad) and Connor (her 6-year old son) by her side. It was one of those moments that will be etched in my mind forever. Incredibly, I thought, I almost missed this glorious moment because of letting my life get in the way and thinking of not coming (you know those many excuses… time, money, my family needing me, etc.).

My own particular Crayola color would have missed out on so much… not only the special moment of the walk down the aisle but also the wedding preparations, meeting the groom, the rehearsal dinner, the dancing at the reception, the late night talks with Linda and Nancy, seeing all the Tessmers, the Shimer Clan, Jan and John, Karen and Jim, as well as winning a prize (grins) and having fun with Linda's Pennsylvania buds Cindy and Carla. It really was priceless. It was an occasion and adventure that makes me really glad to be me.

Who are the people and things that color your world, those individuals that make you laugh while remembering to simply be grateful to be who you are every day? When was the last time you laughed so hard you thought you would bust your gut? Summer it seems is a great time to remember and create fun, to color like crazy and create a picture all your own.

I think along with that fun comes appreciating those people who happen into your life on any given day or at a special occasion… and being very grateful for having them fill up your world with their special color.

So how about trying in the week ahead to create something fun that you have not done in a while? Be adventuresome and creative… be sure to include those people who make you laugh and appreciate you for all that you are… and can be. You may even want to add those people who "bug" you a bit but who add a color all their own. You never know what hidden treasure you may find.

To Your Successes and Victories…

Being vs. Doing

In finding ourselves we realize that we are not human doings but human beings.

~**Dr. Amber Wolf**

Happy Monday,

Here it is, Monday morning, and I don't know about you but in front of me stretches a week accompanied by a to do list that seems to stretch farther than I will have the time to complete it.

Last week looked quite similar, which is why when I heard the words of this week's quote while taking a yoga class (or perhaps I should say squeezing in a yoga class) the words from my yoga teacher rang true. I was being a human *doing* as opposed to *being*, and my goal this week is to change that around as much as possible.

Today is the first day of August; being a Leo, it is my favorite month of the year. The month of my birth and the last essence of summer will happen over the next 30 days. The truth is that I don't want to miss it by doing, doing, doing. While my checked off lists might look good and the accomplishments will feel good, the truth is my inner being won't be feeling very terrific. Well, of course this sounds good in words, but how can I pull it off while still taking care of all I need to do and be, all the while keeping my focus on those things I want to accomplish?… A real dilemma for sure.

I think the reality of keeping somewhat sane is going back to that basic principle of being in the moment whenever we can. Yes, stopping and enjoying the little gifts that are given to us each and every day. So with this week stretching before me, that is my goal. To remember to laugh, breathe (deep and strong), enjoy the simplicity and refreshment of even drinking a glass of water, to enjoy the beauty of a field of sunflowers or the Flatirons as the sun rises on them, to relish a hug from those I love, to walk in the garden or down to the lake with my dog. I will remember to enjoy the little things, and I hope that you can find them too!

What are the small things that make your life enjoyable? Those tiny moments that, if allowed, give you peace of mind and being? My hope for you in the weeks ahead is that you take the extra few minutes necessary to be a human who is being one with yourself. The cool thing is that being present in the moment is available to each and every one of us no matter our age, gender or size of our bank account... it's there if we take the time to appreciate it.

To Your Successes and Victories...

Blazing Inspirations

Vision is the art of seeing the invisible.
~Jonathan Swift

Happy Monday,

The invisible and the unknown lay before us this Monday morning, a blank canvas waiting for us to paint upon it as we look for inspiration to create our world. I had to laugh this morning as, while cruising a few books in my library looking for some inspiration, I happened upon Natalie Goldberg's book, *Thunder and Lighting,* a classic. Amazingly, the chapter I opened to was "Monday Blazes Up Like Gasoline."

What a way to get your week off to a start… with a blaze. As I dragged my kids out of bed this morning I was asked the question, "Why do we have to get started so early?" Well, the truth of it is I did not have an answer except to say that someone, somewhere decided this was the time things would start and we had to go with it.

Yesterday, as we unpacked our many boxes of Christmas "stuff" and listened to Christmas carols, I felt myself careening between overwhelm, nostalgia and a desire to be on an island somewhere. It really amazed me how much Christmas stuff we have collected during our time together as a family. I found myself leaving some of it in the boxes and not really wanting all the clutter of it this year. Oh my… have I gotten humbug about Christmas, have we run out of space, or am I just seeking a more organized life?

The truth is I find that too much "stuff" around me (something that used to charge me up) is now actually smashing my creative juices (not like a fine wine for sure). Yeah, that's it; too much stuff just stops the creative juice flow. Perhaps it's because it is too hard to focus on one thing when there is so much going on. Then I asked myself what to do with all these things that have so many memories attached to them?

The solution I came up with is to create a box for the kids that will hold these memories for them for a future date, allowing us to not be overwhelmed here in the present. Sure, there are things like the Santa head that Travis made, or the angel on a brown paper bag that Bailey made that I cannot let go of at this point (if ever). They must set out for all to see throughout the season, especially as I try and figure out where my babies went and who let these teenagers in the door.

One of the items that inspired me yesterday to hold on to the memories, was picking up the Christmas stocking that I had as a child. My mom had saved it over the years and when I became an adult (not sure when that event happened) she gave me the stocking. Holding that worn out stocking in my hand so many memories of Christmas past flowed into one single feeling of joy and believing, as well as some sadness, for a time never to be again. This red stocking with my mother's beautiful handwriting on it will always be a cherished memory. It gives me the feeling of Christmas in my heart.

So as you head into your week with the holiday season all around you, your blank canvas in front of you, I wish you inspiration to create something special that next week will become a memory to cherish. Keep in mind how memories do indeed create the fabric of our lives.

Here's to blazing inspiration in the week ahead!

To Your Successes and Victories…

Letting Change Happen

We don't see things as they are; we see them as we are.

~Anais Nin

Happy Monday,

Have you ever noticed when change starts to happen it just keeps happening... until you get it right?

Recently, I had someone come over and work with me on getting the Feng Shui flowing in our house. Well, one thing has led to another and I keep making changes in rooms around our home to make them not only work the best for our family but to be aesthetically and functionally pleasing.

You know when you walk into a room and just feel great about being in that space? Well, you know what? When it comes to our rooms one project has led to another and another, and I am finally ready (as is each member of my family) to have it be finished. Though, of course, it will never be completely "done" as that could get too boring.

Sometimes changes can be subtle and sometimes they can be dramatic. Kind of like the change of seasons here in Colorado (going from snow to 100-degree weather). The truth is, sometimes we embrace changes while other times we put off accepting them until the last possible moment. It's important to remember the truly positive results that occur when we allow change to happen. These include but aren't limited to:

- Elimination of stagnation

- Opening our minds to new possibilities

- Creating a new flow of energy

- Forcing us to clear out clutter and cobwebs (literally and figuratively)

- Finding new discoveries about ourselves

- Allowing ourselves and those us around us to communicate in new ways

What kinds of changes have there been recently in your life? What changes would you like to see happen? Take out a piece of paper and write them down. Think about the good that has come or could come from the change. Pat yourself on the back for what you have accomplished or make it a goal and go for it!

The natural energy that arises as seasons change, make it easier for us to create and move with the changes in our lives as well. Why put off until tomorrow what you could do today?

Wishing you a great week and changes ahead!

To Your Successes and Victories…

New Shoes

All the resources we need are in the mind.

~Theodore Roosevelt

Happy Monday,

Well it happened again… Monday has arrived and here I am back home from my trip to L.A. and places beyond. Last week, in between business, visiting some special people and seeing the beautiful Pacific Ocean there came the opportunity to do something that doesn't happen very often… a shopping excursion for shoes.

Now here is my feeling about shoes: While there are some people who will wear just about anything for the sake of fashion, for me, shoes just have to be comfortable or they won't work. My mind shuts down and all I can hear it saying is, "What are you doing to those little toes of yours? All day they must carry you around and here you are putting more pressure on them than they can bear." Alas, there is also something great about the look of a fashionable shoe.

Well, there I was having more time than usual because of being away from home, so I decided to spend the time needed to find just the right pair. With a small budget and a style in my mind for an upcoming event the next day, I began the search for the right pair.

It was funny because I just knew in my gut that the perfect pair of shoes was out there waiting for me to take them home and bring me up a notch in the fashion world. However, during the first hour the shoes were being evasive and then there was just one last hour and one more store to go, a huge shoe warehouse. I tried on a number of shoes in this store thinking, "Come on Cheri you can give a little more to fashion." but a voice inside of me kept saying, "No, hold on to your ideals and you will find that perfect pair."

Heading to the clearance racks I thought, wow – wouldn't it be great if that perfect pair of shoes were on sale! While perusing the shoes, which included some that looked like they belonged in a circus, there, nestled unassumingly in a little box, was "the" pair... just the style I had been looking for with its small fashionable heel. But, I wondered, " Would they keep my feet happy?" Pulling them out of the box and slipping them on my feet I felt like Cinderella for a moment. It had happened; they were the perfect pair of shoes, just the ones that I had been looking for... yes, Victory for my feet!

So ok, you might be saying, that's just fine, Cheri but where are you going with this and why does it matter to me? Well... as these words are appearing on the computer screen I can't help but think about how many times we have the idea of the ideal for something we want in our life, whether it's a small object such as shoes or something more substantial such as a relationship or a job or a place we want to be.

Sadly, it happens that we settle for the uncomfortable pair, the one that is just ok but does not meet all the criteria we had in our mind. Basically, we settle and do not get the reward of getting what we fully wanted. Have you done that lately? Have you given up a want or desire just because it meant putting a little more time into something, looking down one more aisle?

My challenge to you this week is to stop and look at what you are settling for in your life. Where is it causing you pain? What can you do to improve the quality of your life right now, today? For me, wearing this new pair of shoes gives not only my feet a lift but my spirits as well!

Happy shopping for your life's desires in the week ahead!

To Your Successes and Victories...

Victory...
And the Leader

Initiating and Enthusiastically
Embracing Leadership

Belief with the conviction to take to high ground,

Living with purpose, integrity and pride.

Taking the hand of others,

Assisting them on their way,

Determination to make small

and grand differences,

Leading with trust, conviction and purpose.

Do you have the tenacity to lead? Whether in business, in your community, at church or even in your family, if you have the internal strength to lead with tenacity, purpose and a deep sense of caring, it will bless your life and the lives of those whom you touch.

Anyone who stands up and goes after his or her dreams, fighting past the fear in their mind's eye, is a leader. With that leadership comes the resolution to create results. Holding tight to your convictions will allow for you to see the vision of what you want to achieve. At the end of the day, leadership is really about seeing clearly and believing in what you see, for the benefit of those who you care deeply about.

The image of the eagle soaring with the winds makes such a beautiful visual for the role of a true and gifted leader. The strength and majesty magnificence of this beautiful bird truly does portray the spirit of freedom. When you approach leadership from a place of integrity and trust that image of the eagle is you!

A meditation that can engage you fully in the process of leadership is to close your eyes and imagine having a conversation with the leadership heroes who have made a difference in your life. These are the people, living and dead, real and fictional, who have made an impact on your life even if you have never actually met them. I encourage you to try this exercise:

First, as with any visualization, take a couple of minutes to clear your mind as much as possible to all that may be going on around you. Begin by taking a few moments to envision the room that you are sitting in, waiting for your special guests to arrive. Is the room itself large or is it small? Are there windows or no windows? Is it a grand room or fairly plain?

What are the colors of the walls that surround you? Imagine a table where you are seated at, as this is where your leadership heroes will be sitting with you in just a few moments. Is it a wood or metal table? Is it round or oblong? How big is it? How many chairs are there around the table? Are they plain, nondescript chairs, or are they large executive style chairs, chairs that are as magnificent as the people that are about to fill them?

With a clear and detailed vision of the room you are sitting in, you are now ready to have your guests enter. As these people who have made a difference in your life enter the room, ask each to enter one by one. As they enter what is your first impression upon seeing them? What emotions do you feel? What are they wearing, what is the expression on their face? How do you greet them – with a shy handshake, a firm handshake or perhaps with a warm embrace?

As you invite them to join you at the table where do they sit? Repeat this as many times as you have guests who enter the room. Take your time and enjoy the process of greeting them one by one. There is no right or wrong here. You may have one guest. You may have ten. Try to keep it to no more than ten in order to fully focus on their characteristics and individual qualities, otherwise it could get a little crowded!

Once everyone is settled at the table, it is time for you to lead them in a topic of discussion. What will the topic(s) be? Focus on aspects of your life right now that would best be served by their input and guidance. Imagine looking around the table one face at a time as you converse with these special people and the gifts that they have to share with you.

Spend as much time as you need with each guest until you feel the wisdom they share has made a difference for you. This process can take anywhere from 5 minutes, to 15 minutes, to longer if you so desire.

At the end of this exercise make note of how you are feeling. What word/words did you "hear" that made the most difference? Which person sitting at the table stands out in your mind the most? Notice if you feel empowered or just warm and fuzzy. How did you blend in with these special leaders surrounding you at the table? What characteristics of your own matched those of the people at the table? As you draw this important and rewarding meeting to a close what will you take with you that will be most effective for you in your life?

After you have finished this exercise take the time to write down the experience – what you saw… who was there… and the topics of discussion. Keep it in a place where you can refer to it from time to time when you feel that your leadership juju is out of whack.

One of the Master Mind principles outlined by Napoleon Hill outlined focused on the power behind our ability to be leaders. At a recent Victory Circles meeting this was the topic for discussion. Amazingly, some of the strong entrepreneurial women in the room had not considered themselves to be leaders prior to looking at this principle. Engrossed in the day-to-day minutiae of their lives, they had lost awareness of the leadership qualities they possessed in their roles as entrepreneurs, mothers, or even as a volunteers in their community.

As I talk to others about leadership it is always fascinating to me when someone is surprised to be viewed as a leader. Sometimes they get so caught up in just doing what it is they need to do each day; they forget how much they have touched the lives of others in the process. They are just doing what needs to be done. That is a sign of a true leader. It is someone who is not wrapped up in the accolades or power of leadership but, instead, in the process of making the world, even if just their immediate one, a better place to live in.

On the spectrum of opposites, the opposite of a leader is a follower. Not a bad thing to be because without followers there would be no leaders. To effectively lead you need to have proven the ability to follow – to have "walked in the shoes" of those whom you now inspire along the way. By walking down the same, or similar road it enables you to understand what brings them pain as well as what brings them joy. It also helps in the aspect of handling situations and problems as they arise. Think back for a moment to your time around the meditative table we just talked about, and how those leaders left an impression on you just by their mere presence. These are qualities that could not have been absorbed if you hadn't been able to follow.

Many books are published on a fairly regular basis on the topic of leadership. Perhaps, the best resources are biographies and autobiographies of the people that you admire and respect most. Reading their true life stories will deepen your understanding of the road they walked as well as their leadership qualities.

Movies are also a great way also to embrace the strengths of fictional characters who become leaders along the way. Think of those movies that captured your heart with either the strengths or weaknesses of the characters involved. Think of Scarlett O'Hara in *Gone with the Wind*. She had several memorable one-liners which became classics: With the world as she knew it, burning to the ground around her, the devastation of the Civil War – and her own – caused her to cry out, "With God as my witness, I'll never go hungry again!" And then she did what needed to be done as she took the lead.

While there is no doubt that Scarlet was a spoiled and vain woman, there is also no doubt that she carried the mandatory natural leadership skill of strong will. Strong will and determination made it impossible for her to give up. When the going got tough, she amazed everyone around her by shouldering the needs of her family and community. She didn't care who she upset in the process. She knew what had to be done to save them and she did it. Scarlett's leadership skills pushed her to rise to the occasion.

It takes bravery to lead. The Jewish language calls this kind of courage "chutzpa." Leadership is means embracing the human potential and caring deeply about others. Leadership is laughing while you engage others in the laughter as well.

President Dwight D. Eisenhower, the 34th U.S. president, was a leader able to pull together all the arguing egos of the world to greatly assist in bringing peace to Europe during World War II. This was quite a feat for a simple man who came from the small town of Abilene, Kansas. The brilliance of President Eisenhower shone through – and rang true – when he said, "A sense of humor is part of the art of leadership, of getting along with people, of getting things done."

Simply put, leadership is about making the world a better place than it was when you arrived. Enjoy the following Victory Letters as they take you through a variety of thoughts on this critical *Master Mind Principle of Leadership*.

Making a Difference

Kind words can be short and easy to speak, but their echoes are truly endless.

~Mother Teresa

Happy Monday,

And Happy New Year! I hope this first Victory Letter of the year finds you well and putting your best foot forward into your new year with happiness and grace. It is with great joy that I can say my holiday decorations are now all put back into the attic! While I do love the holidays, the amount of work and stress involved can sometimes be overwhelming. This year was no exception. It was exhausting… but with a few long winter naps I am ready to roll into the year ahead.

One of the most enjoyable events of the holiday celebrations was a special afternoon – an now hopefully a new ritual – that I participated in on New Year's Day. My daughter, Bailey, one of my best friends, Nancy; and her sister-in-law, Tanya, took some time out in the late afternoon to share our intentions for the year ahead. The four of us seated ourselves in a quiet corner of Tanya's home and opened ourselves up for the good things that we each wanted for the year ahead. It was an inspiring thing to do and doing it with three people I respect and trust made it all the better. It's something I hope to make a regular routine in the years ahead. (Nancy, that means you have to come to Colorado every year!).

The thought has been with me since two days before the New Year of how important it is to have the support of others when you aspire to do anything in your life. Funny how when you get a strong thought or feeling about something, everywhere you turn you have confirmation in things you read as well as inspirations from people and tools that come your way (such as our New Year's Ritual) showing that you are on the right track.

This year, instead of facing my New Year's resolutions alone, I am looking at how I can achieve what I want in my life by gaining the support of others. Unfortunately, somehow along our way we begin to think (I did for sure) that if we are really strong we must do things on our own. But think about it… those people who have done great things in our world have done it with support, from people who believed in them and the goals they were trying to achieve.

Now think about this… Who are the people who support you in your life such as a mentor, partner or good friend? Those people who you know you can call to help you with anything you might need or who are magically there for you at just the right time? Whether helping you define New Years resolutions, reach personal or business goals, or just lend an ear, these people simply want to see you succeed. Yes, they are the ones who truly want to see you reach happiness and fulfillment. How about the supporters who are in your life to help you achieve a specific goal like a personal trainer or coach?

Who are the people you support? What is the gift that you were given that allows you to support other people? To help them achieve their dreams… Sometimes the little things give the most support in the long run, like how every morning I walk my kids to the school bus. At this point in their life they think I overdo it and only allow me to walk them to our neighbor's mailbox (a good block before the bus stop), but I have not let it deter me as it is a special time for me to wish them a good day and have a moment to talk to them both before the day takes us all away from each other. It is my way of letting them know that I hope their day is the best it can be. It is a small thing, but the small things make the biggest differences.

There is only so much time in the day and we all get filled so quickly with activities that seem to take over our lives. Imagine how you can stop and help someone else to be their best self, to help them through their day… week… year. Indeed I wish you the best in the year ahead with many, many victories to come your way!

To Your Successes and Victories…

Inspiring Fires

Force is all conquering, but its victories are short-lived.
~Abraham Lincoln

Happy Monday,

Last night in honor of my daughter's 14th birthday she had a birthday slumber party that kept her friends and her up and chattering away until 3:00 am. Combine that with a bug I can't seem to knock out and you have someone (me) who is running a bit slow this morning…

Today we find ourselves celebrating President's day by the kids having the day off school. It's funny how times change… remembering when President Washington and President Lincoln both got their own day. Now they have to share. I had a thought this morning (it is amazing that I can think at all) while pondering this week's quote… wouldn't it be kind of cool since we are already blending together two inspiring presidents and leaders to change the day to Leadership Day.

Yes, a day celebrating all those people famous and infamous, past and present, who have been inspiring leaders. Those leaders who didn't need to yell, scream, threaten or use their power in a forceful way to get people moving. People listen to these leaders because they are inspired and passionate about making good things happen. Think about those people in leadership roles who have made the biggest differences in your life.

Sitting here, right now, one of my first bosses comes to my mind. His name was Eric and he was my boss at my first serious job. Perhaps I say serious because it was a job in which I began to see a career path for myself and really felt that my being at that company made a difference. Now here was a man who was my age (the ripe old age of 21), and he inspired me to be the best I could be and really did change the course of my life.

In trying to think about what made him that way I can say probably the one single strength that he possessed is that he was passionate about his work. He led our sales/customer service department with a burning fire inside him to make the company successful. It was also a trickle down effect because the owners of the company, his bosses, gave him the tools and the room (so important) to get the job done.

Now does lack of force mean being nicey-nice all the time? No, it's having people really hear what you are saying... clearly, and with no question of your meaning. Through your leader's efforts you are clear on what it takes to get the job done. I will never forget two weeks or so into that job. I arrived at work about 15 minutes late. Eric walked over to my desk, looked me straight in the eye, and in a clear strong voice said, "Cheri, I just want you to know that it does not work for me or anyone here for you to be late. Do you understand that?" Boy, did I! Now, so many years later, I can remember that moment like it was yesterday. He did not say another word about it and went back to the work at hand. From that day forward I did everything in my power to be on time and not miss any work. I truly loved that job for many years.

So as you move forward in the week ahead think about those people who have led you along your way. Those you now lead... including perhaps your own children.

Do you inspire them by the fires that burn inside of you?

Do you recognize the fires that burn inside of them?

Does your passion and happiness move you, and consequently them, forward?

If not, perhaps you need to re-evaluate what you are currently doing and change course.

If yes, congratulations and keep up the good work! And don't forget to hang out with people who continuously inspire you!

Wishing you a strong week ahead with your passions burning bright!

To Your Successes and Victories...

Faith Forward

Hope is faith holding out its hand in the dark.
~George Iles

Happy Monday,

Last Wednesday I sat in the outpatient clinic at Boulder Community Hospital as they tried to draw blood from my veins. As I sat there, I thought how crazy it was that something so simple for others was such a big deal for me. My veins did not want to let my blood leave my body but my doctor needed to have it for some routine tests to be done.

There was a choice to be made: get up and leave or have faith that with enough poking the nurse would be able to get the blood she needed, allowing me to get my tests done so I could get on with my busy day. I chose to have faith since I had come this far, already having been poked and prodded. Sure enough, before long my blood entered the tube in her hand. Not one who likes the look of blood, I still found myself relieved to see it finally flowing.

As I drove to my next "to do" of the day the thought was in my head – and has remained there most of this week – about how we have choices to accept difficult tasks on a daily basis, and how it's our choice to accept them or not that makes up the life that we live. Good or bad.

Some days, what some would consider the "right" thing to do, is just not a choice we are able to make. Pure and simple, some days we can find ourselves driven to take on every challenge before us and other days we do not. Perhaps that is one of the greatest gifts we have as individuals is to choose what is right for our own well-being on any given day.

Having said that, there is the realization once again that it really comes down to faith. We all have those days when doing what we know will pull us forward seems like walking a long dark tunnel going nowhere (Remember holding your breath when going through a tunnel as a kid?). But then faith comes into play and helps the tunnel get shorter with the light shining brightly at the other end. Perhaps the people, places and things we place in our lives are what assist us in keeping our faith. Here are a few examples:

1. Choosing the people we have around us in our daily life.

2. Utilizing our mentors who are there for us as "backup" when times get overwhelming.

3. Choosing simplicity when it is needed.

4. Keeping our health as a top priority – the healthier we are the clearer we think.

5. Surrounding ours lives with beauty inside and out.

6. Remembering to laugh when it all gets too serious. (Yes, I made joke to the nurse about my used up veins to keep myself from crying, as I am deathly afraid of needles)

7. Reviewing the ways to the means and seeing if the path taken is the best at that moment. Sometimes altering our course even by a slight adjustment makes all the difference in the world.

8. Remembering to breathe.

9. Keeping our head clear about our own purpose for being here on this planet.

10. Appreciating even the little things and giving thanks for our daily bread.

So as you go about the week ahead take a look at your struggles as opportunities to see things just a little bit clearer. If you are running into constant struggles, then perhaps you need to stop and see where your faith got out of sync. Do what you can to get it back, and move forward and learn from each struggle what you can.

Wishing you assistance, as you need it, and the faith to feed it!

To Your Successes and Victories…

Mentoring Magic

Now that your rose is in bloom, a light hits the gloom on the gray.

~Seal

Happy Monday,

This morning's Victory Letter comes to you from the banks of the Animas River here in beautiful Durango, Colorado. We are here over the next few days deciding if this is where our son Travis will spend his college years, starting next September.

It is an interesting adventure when you are about to send your first-born child off into the world. The trepidation centers on how this scholastic decision will affect his entire life. Over this weekend we talked to a variety of people around town about the school and a consistent theme seems to hold true. People continuously said that the biggest asset of Fort Lewis was that the teachers gave a lot of one-on-one time to the students, truly cared, and they actually took on the role of mentoring!

Because the school is smaller, the teachers who tend to come to this part of the world to teach are actually retired from the business or service they now teach, giving this school a different dimensional aspect that is not true in larger colleges. A girl who was serving us dinner last night shared that her marketing professor actually had owned a successful advertising agency and had real world experience in what he was teaching her. All this leaves us excited and hopeful for Travis as we tour the school this morning.

The topic of mentoring and making a difference in someone else's life seems to have been coming up lately. A friend and colleague the other day discussed how to best deal with jerks and the a_h_'s (you fill in the blanks) coming at us on any given day. The truth of the matter is that each morning we wake up with a blank slate in front of us. How we treat other people or allow them to treat us is the one aspect of our life that is totally in our control. People can ruin our day or we can brighten theirs.

Have a snippy and unreasonable boss or perhaps a client who is too demanding and unrealistic? Sometimes we can sit down and have a heart to heart with them on how to change the situation and when that fails sometimes we simply need to walk away. The key is if you feel your stress levels rise when that person enters the room, phones or emails you – you need to do something to change the situation and move forward.

I love this morning's quote from Seal in the lyrics to his song, *Kiss from a Rose*. It's funny how you can listen to a song over and over, not even hearing the words and then suddenly the words ring clear and true for you. Just as these words depict, we can, if we choose be a rose in someone's day – taking away what was previously gray.

We can indeed make a difference in the lives of those we touch in our daily life. What if everyone took on that attitude? Just as we made a worldwide focus to use less energy this past Saturday night – what if we collectively made a focus on giving more heartfelt energy to those whose lives we touch each and every day? Even if we touch their lives for only for a moment, and in passing, by sharing a simple smile.

So as you begin a new week with a clean slate in front of you – think of keeping thoughts of the blooming rose in your mind by making a difference in everyone's life that you touch.

A great quote that I love from Heda Bejar also shares a way to think:

> *"The fragrance always remains in the hand that gives the Rose."*

Your happiness blended with the happiness you bring then becomes your manner of traveling through your day.

Wishing you a week full of a giving and nurturing.

To Your Successes and Victories…

Sacrificing Victories

My hope and prayer is that the sacrifices borne by so many
will spawn and fulfill the promise of our new nation.
~Mel Gibson in *The Patriot*

Happy Monday,

Welcome to Memorial Day... Yesterday was a very wet day so we took time out from the sunshine (because there was none) to watch the movie, *The Patriot*. I did not realize it until the movie began to unfold how appropriate it was to watch this movie on the weekend when we honor and remember all those who have given up their lives for our freedom.

I'm not much of a war movie person, or for that fact much of a war person at all, as the sadness and brutality is way too distressing. But during this movie once again in my life I had a strong realization about all the families that have been affected by our gaining the simple yet complex ideal of freedom. While most of us are focused on our current sufferings in Iraq, all the wars our nation has suffered in its short history are remarkable.

So today in remembering the victories of your life one cannot help but to think of all of those who made each victory possible. Today is the day to remember to say thank you to all those who are responsible for keeping us safe and able to live our lives to the fullest. While evil is out there I know I sleep better at night because of those who are willing to put their lives on the line to keep us safe. Of course 9/11 was our most recent reminder about just how precious and delicate our freedom is to us every day. It reminded us just how many people right here in our country work everyday to keep us safe including our police and fire men and women.

There is a special courage as well as an incredible belief and fortitude that makes these people do what they do by facing life and death dangers every single day. I do thank God that we are blessed to have these people on this Earth who are willing to protect each of us, even at the cost of their own lives. A huge thank you goes out also to their families for the sacrifices that they are forced to make as well. I so hope that those families can find peace in the sacrifices of those they love.

My wishes to you in the week ahead are of remembrance and thankfulness.

To Your Successes and Victories…

Respectable Ideals

I know in my heart that man is good.
That what is right will always prevail and triumph.

~Ronald Reagan

Happy Monday,

Happy Flag Day as well to you! This past week was an amazing one for watching leadership in action as we buried our former president, Ronald Reagan. I found myself intrigued with the ceremonies of the week that unfolded.

One of the things that stood out the most was that the normal political bad-mouthing disappeared when we focused only on the greatness of a man who had served his country. And had served it well. Throughout the week we were able to see the finest aspects of his life and our country, showing reverence and respect.

On our drive to California we listened to the day's activities leading up to and the memorial service on the radio. Upon our arrival we watched the burial service on TV. I was deeply moved not only by the words of his family but the caring of the many leaders of our world that sat shoulder to shoulder paying their respect.

Respect… perhaps it all does come down to that key ingredient. Respect is a wonderful thing to give and to be given. Respect helps each of us grow. Truth is that you can't force it and it is the difference between good leadership and bad leadership. Respect does not mean you have to agree with all of someone's ideas but instead, their ideals.

In your world, who are among the people you respect?

Who makes your world a better place?

When your eulogy is read, what will be said about you?

How much did you care about others? Did you step up to the plate and try and make a difference?

Yes, imagine it, your life has been lived out and everyone you have touched has come to pay his or her respects to you. Who will be there? What will they have to say? Will it be acknowledged that you did all you could to have a good life? Did you take care of others? Did you make a difference? Is the world a better place because you were born?

I hope this gives you some food for thought as you go about the week ahead. No, we probably won't "bring down the wall" or have our names be known to every household in America but what difference can you make in your own backyard, especially for the people you care about and who care about you?

Wishing you a week of respect and kindness as you show your leadership skills along the way.

To Your Successes and Victories...

Every Day Courage

The ultimate measure of a man is not where he stands in moments of comfort and convenience, but where he stands at times of challenge and controversy.
~Martin Luther King Jr.

Happy Monday,

Happy Birthday U.S.A.! Hard to believe that only 229 years have come and gone since those guys, you know… George, Ben, Thomas and all involved in the process, had the courage and the vision to create the foundation for our country. As I write this morning's letter, firecrackers are already once again filling the air.

Several weeks back I asked the question, who the greatest American was or is? Thanks to those who replied. Here are a few of my favorite responses that I would like to share with you on this special day…

I was delighted to hear from my 7th grade teacher Mrs. Carey, who said, *My favorite American is Eleanor Roosevelt. She stood up for what she believed in – helping the poor and blacks when it was not a popular position to speak out about. Even after she was no longer the "First Lady", she worked at the United Nations to form a position on "Human Rights" – She was not beautiful in appearance, but her desire to help humanity made her respected, loved and unfortunately disliked and made fun of – She saw the need to help and did her best to make life better for so many.*

My Mom shared, *My favorites are Thomas Jefferson who at a young age wrote the Declaration of Independence, Harry Truman who was a "real" person and stood his ground not looking for popularity but making the best decisions for our country and John F. Kennedy who was another great President in times of stress.*

Leslie had to say, *my favorite American is Ronald Reagan – because he restored the country's pride in being Americans and was a believer in the free enterprise system!*

While Jeff shared, *there have been so many great Americans, how can I possibly pick only one. Lance Armstrong comes to mind, of course as he heads into the start of* the Tour de France this weekend hopefully winning his 7th Tour title. But let me throw one out that might come as a surprise to you. His name is Bill Wilson. Who's that you say? He is the founder of Alcoholics Anonymous. I believe he has done a great service to humankind by starting an organization that has helped millions of people.

But I have to say my favorite words came from my colleague and friend, Patti Weaver:

My favorite American is the 'average Joe'… the school bus driver that gets kids to and from school safely.

The nurse who makes your friend feel more comfortable during a time of uncertainty or just for a regular check up.

The waitress who brings butter to your table three times and still flashes a smile.

The guy at the coffee shop who has my skinny latte, one Splenda half made before I walk in the door

The produce guy who mentioned that he was about to bring out a fresh box of broccoli if I had time to wait.

The beautician who knows how crazy my schedule is and does her best to squeeze me in when I need to travel within two days.

The friend who goes out of their way to drop off your child at home and saves you an hour so you can pick up your other child.

The janitor who is willing to clean up after others.

The soldier in combat who is seen as a hero by many, but is just an average Joe who was willing to make an incredible career choice.

The dedicated teacher who is so excited about watching kids grow over the course of the year and who cries the last day of school as the kids say goodbye.

The volunteer coaches for Special Olympics athletes.

This list could go on and on… I have a great deal of respect for those who service others everyday and make our lives in many small ways more enjoyable and tolerable."

Thank you Patti for helping us remember the people who make America work for us each and every day, caring about us individually even when their day may not be going so well.

I hope this day and week ahead gives you moments of reflection of all those who have come before us as well as all those today that make our world a better place to be.

God Bless America!

To Your Successes and Victories…

Room at the Top

Our greatest weariness comes from work not done.
~Eric Hoffer

Happy Monday,

As I sit here writing this week's letter not only am I amazed by how time zips by as we enter the last month of summer vacation, but also all the things left to be done before school starts again. Of course, it is best to stop and look at what has been done… as the saying goes… *to accentuate the positive.*

That sometimes can be a difficult task when you look at leadership (the topic of this week's letter) and what has and has not been accomplished by a leader that you have put your trust into. This past week we got our first strong taste of the decisions in front of us in making choices about our country's leadership in the months ahead. While some voices have been strong about making a change in leadership because of what has not been done (peace, economy, etc.), I still am struggling with making a change because it is the only other choice. I guess you could say that I am still reviewing my options.

When it comes time to make a change in leadership, I find that it helps to really think through our choices in finding victory in our world as well as in our own backyards. Today's quote grabbed my eye because it is frustrating for sure when someone says they are going to do something and then they don't. We have all experienced it at one time or another. Even an explanation of why it wasn't done does not ease the loss of faith or disappointment. Indeed, depending on the severity it can make us lose our faith in that person for a long time to come, sometimes without the ability to regain the respect once held for that individual.

Let's face it, when you think of great leaders they are the ones who said they were going to do something and they did it. They took their role as a leader far beyond what was even expected of them as they exceeded expectations.

Nearly two weeks ago I was driving across the state of Kansas in route to Kansas City, Missouri and stopped in the town of Abilene. It is a great way to break up the drive, I have found on previous car trips, by stopping to visit the presidential memorial of Dwight Eisenhower. The memorial includes his presidential library and the chapel which housese his and Mamie's final resting place. This location is built around the home where President Eisenhower and his brothers grew up.

I remember him as a man of greatness accomplishing many things during his presidency. Is it because he is now only a memory and the press has nothing to pound on him about that has made him a great leader or was he one indeed? How about Harry Truman, Franklin Roosevelt, Abraham Lincoln and even George Washington? Would they be elected again today? It compels me to pull out the history books and again read about these men who shaped our country.

Perhaps the best way to look at leadership is how we ourselves get things done. So many of us are in a role of authority in our life in one-way or another. We can play a leadership role in the work we do, the community we live in or even in our own home. So what are some key roles and strengths in finding Victory in leadership? Here are 5 of each that I think really make a difference... hope you think so too.

Key Roles that make a leader shine...

COMMUNICATOR – the ability to share your thoughts and the thoughts of those you lead clearly, accurately, effectively and precisely. Get inside their heads and help them get inside of yours.

PEACE KEEPER – keeping the peace. Picking battles carefully and wisely... better yet, avoiding them all together by resolving situations as they arise.

MOTIVATOR – Even on the days when a leader is down they must raise the spirits of those around them to help them see the goals and the good for all. Be the light at the end of a tunnel, the voice in the dark.

VISIONARY – The ability to see as well as create tomorrow and way beyond. The extra ability to see other's visions and incorporate them into your own makes you a leader people want to be around. It's important to make them feel part of the process.

CAREGIVER – A great leader is the one people go to in times of trouble, if not always, for a solution at least to help ice the injuries of the day.

Key Strengths include but certainly are not limited to…

COURAGE – It certainly is not always easy to be in a Leadership position. Most of the time you are swimming against the tide. Always to being the calm in the storm no matter how crazy the storm might get is key to being a successful leader.

STRONG BELIEF – Unwavering, holding true to the cause…

COMPASSION – Holding close the ability to listen and learn from those around you. Not allowing your self to come to unfavorable conclusions about others to quickly.

LOYALTY – Holding true to those who have belief in you.

HONESTY – Taking the time to honor the trust that has been placed with you and not wavering from that truth.

As you move about your week and think of leadership changes you would like to see come about… stop and look at yourself… are you the best leader you can be? Remember the words of Daniel Webster who said, "There is always room at the top."

To Your Successes and Victories…

CHAPTER 5

Victory...
And Imagination

Creating Inspiration to
Continuously See What is Not

Never before seen except in my mind's eye.

Freedom to create is a blessed thing to have and hold.

Reaching for something that will allow me to give of myself,

As I watch something new and exciting unfold!

Have you ever thought about the capacity of your imagination? What comes into your mind as you think about it now? Do you envision a blank piece of paper and the possibility of what can go on it? Or does your mind wander to something else entirely?

The little girl alive and well in me loves to think about the fairies hanging out in my garden. I love to imagine how they'll enjoy each plant and trinket I've chosen to put into it. My garden then enhances my ability to imagine and inspires me to do all the hard work required to create it. It does not become work at all at that point. It becomes a passion.

Passion is what drives us to do so many things in our life with joy and grace. With the power of our imagination as our fuel, how can we go wrong? Combined with time and tenacity the things we imagine can in fact become real. We imagine something to exist before it actually does – and then before we realize it, that which we imagined is then suddenly a real and tangible thing!

In his book, *Laws of Success,* Napoleon Hill believed the principle of imagination to be one of the most important skills we have to lead us towards success in our lives. Recently while writing on this topic for the Victory Circles I was reminded how much I enjoy the process of developing ideas, going through the planning process and imagining how it will enrich the businesses of our members. In other words, I love to imagine not only my victories but also the victories of others. The process of watching those ideas take on a life of their own is, well, magic!

Walt Disney is probably one of the most famous imaginers of our time, so much so that he called his staff at Disney his *Imagineers.* He was able to imagine and inspire those around him to create not only the wonderful characters of his stories, but also a physical place that he dubbed, *the happiest place on earth – Disneyland.* For anyone who has ever felt the magic of walking down Main Street USA in Disneyland, you actually have felt the magic of Walt's imagination. No matter how many times I went as a kid (and I went a lot growing up in Southern California), it held the same magic for me each and every time.

As a kid, I always found it hard to sleep the nights before going to Disneyland. Once I arrived, I had a whole joyous day in front of me to live the magic. So many wonderful experiences at the park make up a big part of my childhood, thanks to a man who allowed his imagination to fully come to life. Imagination is a power that each of us possesses but then we must choose whether or not to move forward with what comes into our mind, allowing those ideas, thoughts and dreams become a reality.

Think back in time and visualize your fondest childhood memory. Think of yourself as that little girl or boy and remember what it was that brought your imagination to life. Did you play with baby dolls or Barbie, creating imaginary life situations for her and Ken? Or did you create battlefields out in the backyard or field near your home? Did you love to swim and create underwater adventures as you cruised through the magic blue waters during the summers of your childhood? Maybe you jumped on your bike and headed to parts unknown – excited about the possibilities before you.

I can remember as a young child going to what my brother and sisters and I had dubbed the "Penny Candy Store". Remarkable as it seems today, my dad would give each of us a "whole" dime and tell us to jump in the back of his Chevy pick-up truck because he was taking us to the penny candy store. We were in heaven because we would start to imagine the choices we'd make when we got there. Each piece of candy cost one penny (thus the name we gave the candy store) giving us ten sugary and delicious choices to make!

Walking into the store, there it was – the large glass display counter where from the front we could gaze at all the possibilities for satisfying our sweet tooth. It seemed like it was ten feet high but in reality I think it was more like five. All the candy we could imagine existing in the whole world was right there for us to take. We made our choices slowly and carefully knowing the hours (or maybe minutes) of enjoyment those beautiful sweet treats would bring to us. Whether it was a Lick-a-Maid candy packet, long red string licorice, gum or one of so many other choices, it was our choice. Riding home in the back of my dad's pick-up, the wind blowing through our hair and our bag of candy in hand – we were happy kids. Our imaginations, touched with a bit of reality made the journey to the penny candy store even sweeter.

When and where did your imagination fully come to life? Who were the people who helped in the process of bringing it to life? Who were your imagination buddies, or as Walt would call them, your fellow *Imagineers*? How many hours did you spend creating something that had never been there before or enhancing something to make it better? How often did you allow yourself to fully submerse all your thoughts into doing only that one activity? Past and future thoughts melted away because you were in the zone of doing what you loved to do. You were living in the moment. Yes, you were enjoying the full potential of your life in those moments.

As you continue to visualize, think about what you were able to create during this time that made your life special. Really focus on the feeling of what you felt, the energy that coursed through your body, the joy and radiance that beamed from you. The exciting part of thinking about imagination is remembering that while it is a skill easily accessed by children – the process can be just as easy for adults if we open ourselves up to what is possible. Unfortunately, sometimes we get a little too stuck in "reality" and lose sight of what we could potentially make possible from what currently does not exist.

When you hear people speak about their creations, you may also hear a hint of familiar childlike excitement. If you have ever heard Steve Jobs of Apple Computer fame announce a new product you know what I mean. When he introduced the revolutionary iPhone – he was like a kid in the proverbial candy store. I was excited not only for myself at the possibility of getting one, but also excited for him and his team for creating such an innovative new product.

Imagination was the driving force behind my decision to create the Victory Circles.

I had known for many years in my role as a business coach that I loved the interaction and results that come from group coaching. I also knew that the Master Mind principles that Napoleon Hill had first introduced were of great interest to me. I wanted to experiment with them to see what would unfold. What was also true for me was the desire to create something new in my life, something that would incorporate my love for working with entrepreneurs. The seed of the idea had been germinating for a couple of years. Finally, in January of 2006 enough good ideas came together, and in a short period of time the first Victory Circle was created!

With the premise of like-minded women as a guiding light I started to ask women entrepreneurs whom I knew, to come join me on the last Friday of that March as a member of the first Victory Circle. It resonated with many, and on the day of our first meeting, I was touched and delighted by the electricity that was sparking throughout the room. It was an idea that was working and working well. The Victory Circle – an idea that came to life in my imagination – was born.

Over the course of the past five years that Victory Circle has grown to incorporate more Circles facilitated by other entrepreneurially minded Business Coaches. The spark has become a flame much to my delight. We have added to the depth and breadth of what the Circles offer, as we listened to the imaginations of others and what they saw as ways to enhance their Victory Circles membership. Seeing the organization grow is an experience I will never forget in my lifetime. It is also my hope that none of my fellow "Victory Sisters" will ever forget the experience either, as we continue to learn and grow together.

When we first addressed the Master Mind principle of Imagination in the Victory Circles – I created an exercise (yes, from my imagination) that would allow us to tap into the essence of the Inner Child who still is alive and well in each of us. It was designed to spark in us the child we once were and the joys we once felt. I really wanted something that would remove all the day-to-day realities and dealings of life and work in order to focus solely on the imaginations of the Circle members. I was delighted by their response.

The ladies opened themselves up to remember things about the little girls they once were. They discovered that they, in fact, could connect the dots of their lives and bring some of those childhood imagination skills forward, and use them in their lives as women today.

We had a great discussion about playing out in the street as children and coming home when the streetlights were turned on. One member remembered a fact she had long-forgotten, in that her favorite color as a child was yellow, something she left the meeting wanting to reincorporate into her life. Another member shared how doing the exercise moved her to call her grandmother and thank her for some wonderful memories from her childhood – something she had never done before and was grateful she could still do.

It seemed appropriate to share that exercise with you here and now to see what comes to life for you. Keep in mind that I have changed the gender references so that you of the male persuasion reading this book can benefit from this exercise also. Enjoy!

Exploring Your Imagination

Our imaginations began to percolate early in our lives. Think back to when you were a little girl or boy. Think of things you loved and the passion with which you loved them. Remember your excitement in the things you were discovering about yourself and the world around you, how they carried you forward each day.

Ask yourself these questions about that time in your life:

- How did you love to spend your time?

- What was your favorite game to play?

- Who were the friends who brought you the most joy?

- What was your favorite story?

- Who was your favorite storyteller?

- What was your favorite color?

- What was your favorite food?

- What was your favorite thing to wear?

- Who were the family members that "got" you?

- How did find yourself letting your imagination come out to play?

- What are one or two of your fondest memories?

Moving forward to the woman/man you are now, ask yourself these questions:

- How often do you let your little girl/boy come out to play?

- What makes the little girl/boy inside of you smile today?

- Do you incorporate your little girl/boy essence into your power of Imagination?

- Do you move forward and create the things your imagination makes possible?

Take the answers to these questions and share them with someone who can help you to fully embrace them, just as we did in the Victory Circle.

Finally, on this topic of your imagination, allow yourself to fully bring yours to life! Put your little kid shoes on, and open up that mind. Do it as often as you can. You will be delighted at what is possible for you in your life. Some of the greatest minds of our time had a lot to say on the topic and here is just a sampling...

Albert Einstein said:

"Imagination is more important than knowledge."

Pablo Picasso said:

"Everything you imagine is real."

George Bernard Shaw said:

"Imagination is the beginning of creation. You imagine what you desire, you will what you imagine and at last you create what you will."

Henry David Thoreau said:

"The world is but a canvas to the imagination."

Let your imagination come to life as you enjoy the further telling of creativity in the following Victory Letters which center on the **Master Mind Principle of Imagination**.

Your Masterpiece

Lord, grant that I may always desire more than I accomplish.

~Michelangelo

Happy Monday,

Imagine it… you're Michelangelo. You just started painting the Sistine Chapel and you have sooooo much more to get done. It's Monday morning and you are lying there facing the ceiling with your paintbrush back in your hand. You are thinking of the years ahead of you to complete what may or may not be a good gig. You have those telling you that you are insane and those telling you that you have the opportunity of a lifetime in front of you to create something that will be appreciated for generations to come (these people seem few and far between).

You know, there are days when we all wake up and the project in front of us seems like the never-ending story. You begin to question yourself and what the path is that you are really supposed to be on. Each of us has our own little ingredients that are added to the pie that makes up our world. Those of us of the female persuasion get to have an extra jolt of hormone restructuring added to the pie every month just for a little added flavor.

This past weekend my daughter celebrated her 12th birthday with a slumber party of her close girlfriends. She asked me beforehand, to please make myself scarce… except when needed. As I found myself in the role of someone only wanted around when requested… you know, to serve the pizza… cake, etc., it made me realize that this was not something I would put up with much beyond this special event. My sanity just cannot handle the "speak when spoken to" treatment. Life needs to be more fun than that kind of treatment allows.

A Victory Letter reader shared with me late last week that feeling of always being the "doing" person and while attending a funeral on Friday asking himself, "Is the 'to do list' enough to fill my days?"

Again, I ask you to imagine your days filled with passion and enjoyment, doing what you want to do. Creating something that did not exist before... Exploring something you had not explored before... Challenging yourself like you never had before... Not putting up with things that don't work for you in your life... Simply put... enjoying yourself like you never enjoyed yourself before! What in the world would that look like for you? Remember that every moment does not have to be great ... but catching the best of each moment sure makes such a difference.

(Author's Note: Are you catching are recurring theme by this point of the book?)

I am finding my years as a parent coming full swing with my children turned teenagers... perhaps better known as my stupid years. I must find a new way to be me while I let my children find themselves... oh, a very challenging role to play. But as with so many things along our way it is a necessary role, one with a strong purpose that requires me to take the journey from here to there.

Perhaps it helps to keep in mind that what today may seem lame, unnecessary, and pointless, indeed it may be the means to the end. What is the long-term picture? Where is the journey really, I mean *really* taking you and me? We need to stop, look and listen to all that is happening around us. Yes, once again our heart needs to lead the way as February winds down to its final week before us.

Enjoy the masterpiece you are creating along the way!

To Your Successes and Victories...

Take on the Fear

Feel the fear and do it anyway.
~Tamara Mellon

Happy Monday,

This past week has been one of those weeks when a variety of life situations presented themselves to me in one form or another. I find myself reflecting on them as I begin writing this Victory Letter to you. As always, my goal is to share these thoughts with you in a quick few minute read.

First, while I did not mention it in last week's Victory Letter, I was delighted to see Reese Witherspoon win the Oscar for best actress. Not only do I love her as an actress, but also there is just a special sweetness about her that I really like. Add to that the role she played to win the award – June Carter Cash, a woman who dealt with many heartaches and fears in her life and just kept on going. It was great in Reese's acceptance speech how she shared the words of June, "I'm just trying to matter". What a great way to look at life through the peaks and valleys that we all go through.

The second event, one that saddened me this past week was the death of Dana Reeves. Now here was a woman who faced more than her share of adversity and fear. Through it all she kept on going with a style and grace that was really beautiful. I remember hearing her talk on Larry King in January of '05, a few months after her husband, Christopher Reeves had died, and after also just having to deal with her mother's death. Her strength as she spoke just radiated through her whole being. Her personal views on the "here and now" were so powerful.

Both June Carter Cash and Dana Reeves had a large amount of grief in their lives. But they kept going with a smile on their faces and more importantly in their hearts. They lived their lives to the fullest. Really, that is all each of us can do. They were both powered by the strong love they had for the man in their lives, the love of their lives. This love, in both cases, helped them pull not only themselves up and past their fears, but the men in their lives, Johnny Cash and Christopher Reeves, were also given the gift of their powerful love.

A bit closer to home, this past Saturday I took my daughter on her first modeling interview. This has been a dream of hers for a long time. We had heard of an opportunity to interview with an agency in Denver and, unsure what it was all about, we went for it. I really wanted this to be a learning experience for her no matter how it turned out. One thing we talked about on the drive to Denver was about not setting our expectations too high. We also wanted to enjoy the process and remember this was our very first shot at working on her dream.

We ended up having fun as we sat in a room full of parents and kids wanting to be the next big star (sadly, there were some parents who clearly wanted this more than the kids). Bailey practiced the one line she was going to give for the video camera part of the interview and this in itself helped her to realize that at that moment, no matter the outcome, she was living her dream. She was going after something she wanted. She was learning what she needed to do to really live this dream. She knocked down the fear she felt and got the first step of her dream started… knowing that what will come, will come.

One of best things that the gentleman who was running the interviews told us was that if anyone sitting in the that room really wanted to make this dream a reality they needed to want it very strongly because it is not an easy business, full of a lot of rejections, and that those who succeed are the ones who just keep trying. A "No" didn't mean never. You had to love what you were doing and keep going!

Oprah said that, "Luck is just preparation meeting opportunity" (a quote from Seneca). As we move into this week of the Irish and St. Patrick's Day, maybe one of the things we need to remember in preparing ourselves everyday is to look past our fears and do it anyway. To be prepared to matter, not only to others but maybe most importantly to our selves, remembering that today needs to matter just as much as tomorrow and the next and the next…

Wishing you a week full of magic and delight as you enjoy each and every moment, taking on the fear you meet along the way and doing it anyway! You never know what special little leprechaun you may meet along your way!

To Your Successes and Victories…

Re-adjusting the Canvas

Make each day your Masterpiece.
~Joshua Wooden

Happy Monday,

Honor – It seemed to be the theme that kept coming up during last night's Academy Awards presentations. Honoring your work and the people who you depend on each day to bring your masterpiece, whatever it is, to life. I loved what Alan Arkin had to say upon winning his Oscar. He shared that it was the sense of teamwork and family that made every day on the set of *Little Ms. Sunshine* a joy.

The joy that they experienced on the set of *Little Ms. Sunshine* helped them to create their masterpiece. Here was a little movie that became a big hit because of the people involved in it, from the actors to the production crew, people were able to feel their vision.

There was a point in my life when I dreamed of being a famous actress. For years, I attended a drama class one day a week at a beautiful old arts center with my best buddies, Linda, Nancy and Susan. The adventures we had before and after class as we walked there from our regular day school, Our Lady of Lourdes, were almost as fun as the performances we put on. I thought for sure we were all destined to become famous actresses but life took us in different directions.

I now realize that those days helped to establish our creativity and imagination, something I hope that we never lose sight of on our journeys. I am also happy to report that the friendships also remain strongly intact after over 40 years, even with each of us now spread across the U.S.

There are some of you reading this morning's letter who are soloprenuers like myself, some who have built your companies up with a number of employees and some working for larger organizations. In either case it is important to surround yourself with people who are just as interested in your success as they are their own. That is what makes a winning team.

It's funny that the Academy Awards have become infamous for winners getting asked to leave the stage by the music cutting off their speech because they cannot stop thanking the people who helped in getting them to that stage in the first place.

So as you move forward to create your masterpiece this week take a look around you. If you were to win an Academy Award tomorrow for the work that you do, who is it that you would thank? Who are the important people who would make you kick yourself if you forgot to mention their names in the one or two minutes you would have?

When was the last time you actually did thank them for the contributions they make to your life? They could either be employees, colleagues, clients, or vendors, or someone who cares enough about you to support your daily efforts in creating your masterpiece.

Showing your thanks is your way of honoring the value they add to your life.

So as you move forward in your week ahead, don't lose sight of how important your work is not only to you but also to those around you. Create for yourself and for them. If your work starts to look like less of a masterpiece and more of a chore you dread – maybe it's time to readjust your canvas. Remember, we only get one shot at this lifetime – shouldn't we grab every opportunity available to be all we can be?

Happy Painting!

To You Successes and Victories…

Color Your World

What color would you paint your life?
~Sotheby's

Happy Monday,

I hope this Monday morning finds you enjoying some colorful Easter eggs and perhaps even a little chocolate! Easter is now behind us and flowers are popping up everywhere… spring is indeed in full swing.

This week's quote was in a magazine ad I saw that portrayed a beautiful island beach setting with just those simple words. "What color would you paint your life?" The blue-green of the waters against the pure sandy beaches made me just want to jump into the picture and find myself walking along the shore of that beach. The caption really opened my thinking to how indeed I want to continue with the colors that make up the painting of my life.

I found myself asking the question, "What brush strokes would it take to make me happy, satisfied and even joyous in the days, weeks, months and years that stretch before me?" What would your brush strokes look like?

One of the things I came to realize in this past week is the importance of painting from your gut. I think that is what some of the great past and contemporary artists have done. How many times has your mind worked together with your gut and heart telling you something? Something that affected your life in a tremendous way! Even in the smallest ways…

While walking through my yard a few days ago I noticed some tree seedlings dropping on the grass. They were unfamiliar to me until I realized they were coming down from our cottonwood tree. As I looked up at the tree I was amazed by how big and healthy it had become over the past few years. This tree was such a part of our backyard when we moved into this house thirteen years ago and about five years ago it had begun to look pretty sparse and not so healthy. We called in a tree guy who told us it was diseased and the only thing to do was to cut it down.

Well, there was something about that tree that just would not allow us to cut it down. It had a strength and character that had become a part of our backyard and we weren't ready to let it go. Our gut and heart said to not heed the words of the tree man and let the tree live. I guess in our mind's eyes we painted it healthy. In addition, we removed some branches to help it live. Well, live it has, growing probably another ten feet in the process. Healthier than ever! So as of this writing, it is ready to color our backyard even greener this spring and summer.

Is there something in your world that you have been hesitating to paint? Has your gut and heart been telling you to do something and you have been choosing to either ignore or put off thinking much about it until... tomorrow? What if you picked up your paintbrush today and began painting the image of what you wanted something in your world to look like? How would it color your world?

We are indeed the sole artists responsible for the beauty of our own life. If we put the paintbrushes away and forget to inject the color into our world... perhaps we just start living in black and white or monotone colors! How boring and drab would that become for us? What would we be missing? What would we never create... even if in our own mind?

I wish you bright colors in the week ahead as your paintbrush forges you ahead!

Happy painting!

To Your Successes and Victories...

Beating the Odds

Not all who wander are lost.

~Bumper Sticker

Happy Monday,

Well, okay… indeed by now it is Happy Tuesday… funny in that this week's letter is about overcoming obstacles and yesterday I had series of computer obstacles that delayed this weeks letter by one day… enjoy!

How true this week's quote is… in so many ways. I saw it while driving through Boulder last week and it put a smile on my face. Ironically, a few days later I was at my friend Deb's hair salon taking care of those things she only knows for sure… and she shared with me a story from *Bicycling Magazine* about a spunky woman, Annie Cohen Kopchovsky.

As this true story went, in June of 1904, this spirited 5'3", 100-pound woman took off from Boston to circle the world on a bicycle. Yes, a 40-pound bicycle (though she later exchanged it for a much lighter one… 20 pounds)! A $10,000.00 bet that would support the woman's suffrage movement as well as the notoriety she would gain to accelerate her writing career were the two pieces of motivation that got her on her journey. She had quite the adventure while she was out wandering around.

Another compelling aspect of the bet was that she had to go penniless with only the clothes on her back. She found ways to get money from sponsors that took on her cause all along the trek.

Her story is inspiring when you think of the "things" in us that start the "whine" factor on why we can't do something or achieve something in our lives. She crossed oceans (the only time she was allowed not to bicycle) and the major continents of the world, arriving back home by the 15-month deadline that was placed on her. The most amazing part was she had only learned to ride a bike two days before her journey began! Sure, she crossed obstacles along her way but she kept going, which is what brought her the ultimate success.

I love stories of people who have beat the odds. Somehow it helps when the odds are set high before us... to look back at those who have wandered before us in our lifetime. Over the weekend this idea hit home even more for me when we rented the DVD *Finding Neverland*, the story of J.M. Barrie and how the story of Peter Pan unfolded before him as he let his mind and imagination wander to places no one had ever been before.

The writer in me was inspired... could I dare go to such places? The thought is intriguing. One thing I think that both Annie and Mr. Barrie had in common was that they were driven by their passion and belief that they could do what lay before them. Interestingly enough, they both accomplished these major achievements at the start of the 20th century when there was far less technologies for them to accomplish what was in their minds eye. Perhaps indeed less was and is more.

When it all comes down to it, where would you like to wander? Where could you go that would bring forth your gifts while you had an adventure? I dream of visiting Italy and writing in a villa overlooking the sea... of accomplishing things in my day-to-day life today that will take me and my family there. Can I accomplish such things... can you?

It has been said that if you want something badly enough you can make it happen. You move forward past the obstacles along the way and make your adventure happen. Belief in your self is probably the most difficult and yet the single most important factor, especially when those obstacles and major changes in the road get in our way.

In this week ahead let yourself dream... write your dreams down and look at what seemingly impossible challenges you can accomplish. No, it doesn't mean you have to circle the world on a bike or write a children's classic story. However, it does mean you have to open your self up wide to the possibilities of what you possess inside of you. Perhaps when things go wrong we are not lost... it is just part of our journey. I wish you happy wanderings!

To Your Successes and Victories...

Pursuing Enthusiasm

Nothing great was ever achieved without enthusiasm.
~Ralph Waldo Emerson

Happy Monday,

Just how enthusiastic are you feeling this Monday morning? About your life, your job, and your business or just about anything you are doing in your life? I hope the answer is a resounding "very enthusiastic." It is interesting how the level of enthusiasm for what we are doing either makes it a chore or a labor of love.

This past weekend I turned 47 years old. Amazing. Was I enthusiastic? Well… what choice did I really have? The presents and the attention (along with the fact that I am still alive) were nice, so I guess it makes up for the fact that my sweet 16-birthday party becomes further and further in my past.

We all know someone who gets too wrapped up with his or her age. But you know that hair coloring commercial is true: we are not getting older we are getting better. What the body may not show (or shows too much of) the mind makes up for ten-fold, like the lessons we have learned, the people who have come and gone, the whole mystery of life unfolding before us each and every day.

I participated in a great conversation on Friday during a talk I gave for a regional convention of an international non-profit organization. The discussion revolved around building your sales muscle. We discussed how everyone is a sales person in one way or another in his or her life – especially if we are living, working or participating in activities with other human beings in which we want to share our thoughts and possibilities for how things could be, or how you would like them to be.

One of the top strengths in a good sales person is enthusiasm. If you do not believe in what you are sharing you begin to feel like the "used car salesman," saying anything to get a customer or client to agree with what you want and not care how it may adversely affect them. Truth is that too much of this approach will not only turn people off but also cause your enthusiasm to die because there is nothing sparking it along the way.

Enthusiasm – it's that burning desire we see this week in each of the athletes who have made it to the Olympics. Is it true that those who win gold, silver or bronze have more enthusiasm than the others? Is their enthusiasm so strong it helps them fine-tune their sport and to become the best in their type of sport? An interesting concept to ponder…

The great thing about enthusiasm is that no matter how others try to squish it, if it is strong it just keeps ticking along making us even more determined as each day passes. It puts a smile on our face when we need it the most. We keep it on the forefront of our mind, the freshness in the start of a project or job, making sure to keep it all the way through. Look at people who have successfully been doing something for years and years. Their enthusiasm shows. In order for enthusiasm to continue to kindle I believe the following components are necessary, and I am sure you could think of a few more:

Belief – Enjoyment – Satisfaction – Success – Empowerment – Teamwork – Energy

As this week unfolds I wish you lots of enthusiasm to pursue what you are doing. If indeed you find yourself without any enthusiasm, perhaps you should take a look at what you are doing and find a way to change or enhance your course. In a gift I once received were these words by Emily Dickinson: "Success is counted sweetest, by those who ne'er succeed, to comprehend a nectar, requires sorest need."

Have a great week finding your nectar!

To Your Successes and Victories…

Music Therapy

I can almost hear the echoes of the past, from the voices of the years gone by so fast. I'm using all my might to try and find the light in the Milky Way tonight. It seems our hopes and dreams were a million miles away, the worlds not what it seems and it's changing everyday.

~Graham Nash

Happy Monday,

I hope this Labor Day finds you enjoying some time off and if it is Tuesday before you read this then the wish is here that you had a terrific and relaxing weekend. Labor Day, the day we appreciate the men and women of our country who work. Can you imagine spending 30+ years of your life producing a product that brings a smile to millions of people's hearts? This was my thought last Thursday night as we sat at Red Rocks enjoying the sounds of Crosby, Stills and Nash (CSN).

Now of course, not only is the Red Rocks Amphitheatre my favorite music venue of all time but CSN brings back to me the wonderment of my youth and the strength in their special blend of music that has stood the test of time. So there we sat on a beautiful summer night, a gentle breeze blowing, watching these three men who affected my life in many ways and yet they don't even know who I am. In fact, I once dated a guy simply because he looked so much like Stephen Stills (proved not to make for enough of a substantial relationship).

When Graham Nash began singing the words used in this week's quote from a song from his newly released album with David Crosby, it gave me goose bumps and brought a little tear to my eye. Sitting there watching the nearly full August moon with Ed by my side, I realized that a new memory had just been created, enhanced by the beauty of my surroundings and the beautiful music. While those three men who were standing on that stage singing and playing some incredible guitar have changed physically quite a bit (so had the people in the audience!)… the music was just as beautiful as it was all those years ago.

Beautiful music has the power to allow us to recall our best selves while taking the good out of the bad… leaving just the pleasant memory. I mean, let's face it, I was 13 or 14 when I first started listening to CSN during some pretty turbulent years in my life. Dealing with coming of age in the early seventies, my parents had divorced and then both remarried. I moved to a new town and had to leave my childhood buddies – but the music remained a constant. Something I knew I could count on. It went with me wherever my journeys took me. It always seems to know where to go in my heart.

It is interesting that as I was writing this letter I hopped over to the internet and looked up "music therapy" and did you know that there is an association that has been around since the 70s that supports music therapy used in medical situations including Alzheimer's patients. Insurance in some states even covers it.

So here is your assignment this week… pull out some music you have not listened to in a long time… if it is still on an 8-track you may have to catch up with the times. In fact, I am still amazed at how you can now, through the glory of technology, download single songs (yes, legally – let's give the musicians their hard earned dollars). Find that song that touched your heart one summer night, the day you fell in love, the day you fell out of love, during a good time with a special friend, or simply while cruising in your car.

Let the music be around you to help reduce the stress of your world. Think about how massage therapists always play music to help in that whole relaxing experience. They do it because it works. Whether you like rock or pop, classical or opera, don't let a day go by that you don't have some kind of music fill your heart and, yes, I think your soul.

Happy rocking to you in the week ahead!

To Your Successes and Victories…

Running Away

It's comin' on Christmas, their cuttin' down trees, their puttin' up reindeer for my baby and me. Oh, I wish I had a river I could skate away on.

~Joni Mitchell

Happy Monday,

Several times last week I heard from people who wanted to just skate away and not return. The craziness of the season was getting to them. I was asked to run away with these people who are near and dear to my heart and for a moment or two it sounded somewhat appealing.

One of them, my sister, reminded me of when we were kids and I would pack up my dolls and baby buggy, getting ready to hit the road, but never making it past the corner of our street. I asked her to go with me once and she smelled dinner cooking and declined. As a teenager I got a bit more daring and actually had a couple of mini adventures trying to sort out the who and what I was all about. Somehow though, it never seemed to be what I thought it was going to be… perhaps because of the fact that no matter where you go… there you are.

Something that lets me run away right at home is writing. Now some of you I know may be saying, "Oh, I can't write, it is just not in me, I don't have the time, etc." Just remember, writing can take as short as fifteen minutes and it is only for your eyes to read. We all have hundreds of thoughts and words circulating in our brains all the time. It is really wonderful when we put them down on paper and do a free-write – no structure and not caring what anyone thinks. You will be surprised at what will hit the paper or computer screen. Here, I will give you an example and run away on paper for a minute with the thought of skating away as my subject for the writing…

The river lay before me. I had escaped the hustle of the day and snuck away when no one was watching. It was a blue-sky day, my favorite kind of Colorado days. The stillness in the air was electrifying. As I laced up my skates the idea of the smooth ice beneath my feet was exciting. It also was great to think about once I got down the river no one would be able to touch me with requests of any kind. The silence of this moment was just what I needed.

There I was on the ice, picking up speed and loving the moment, the day and the time before me. The sun was shining on my face warming me up nicely from the coolness of the day. Onward I skated in which ever direction I chose. The birds were singing and sending me along on my way. I didn't know where I was going but I was on my way.

Now it's your turn to write about your perfect runaway moment by answering these questions:

If you were to run away, where would you go?

Who and what would you be running from?

What and who would you be running to?

Be sure to describe your feelings in detail and give yourself at least 15 minutes to write. Get it all down on the paper and who knows where you might end up.

As the holidays continue to unfold this week be sure to enjoy the beauty of this season. And keep your skates handy!

To Your Successes and Victories…

CHAPTER 6

Victory...
And a Pleasing
Personality

Bringing Forth the Best of
Your Unique Features and Strengths

You are you,

I am me.

Each with our own special grace,

Let's celebrate the gifts we bring,

Each from our own unique space.

Most likely every morning upon waking up, the same person is usually there looking back at you in the mirror. Yes, it is you! Over the years, the image that you have been looking at may have changed … just a bit. A bit more maturity may be evident on the face of the person looking back at you, but no doubt about it – that is you staring back.

Actually, if you stop and think about how many times you have looked in the mirror over the years the transition and change you have witnessed is amazing. Remember barely even being able to reach the bathroom mirror? The first mirror I can remember gazing into was in a bathroom with pink tiles. Pushing the stool in front of the sink to get a glimpse of what my mom and older siblings were seeing, brought me to the amazing moment of staring back at myself with my curly brown hair popping out from all sides!

The sixth chapter of this book is all about taking what you have learned in the previous five, and seeing how you can fully and regularly embrace your life. We have talked about the entrepreneurial spirit, self-confidence, leadership, creating habits of self-control with money as you gained a deeper understanding of saving money and honoring your time. In the last chapter as well, I hope that you really began to fully get your arms around your uniqueness as you delved into your imagination. Which of these principles has resonated most with you to this point? What do you find yourself wanting more of? What ideals seem specific to you? How have these Master Mind principles touched the core of who you are? How have the corresponding Victory Letters begun to help you see yourself in a better light?

At this point in the book we are going to think more about reflecting inwards towards the unique and inquisitive personalities that make each person on this planet special in their own way. Can you visualize your own personality? Can you write about it? Do you enjoy spending time with yourself? How often do you engage in conversations with yourself?

It is interesting to think about how we appear to be just one person most people view on the outside. In reality, there are many personalities hanging out within our inner psyche. In other words, within us, it takes a village of personality types to make up the whole package of who we have become, not only through our DNA make-up, but also through our unique life experiences. These can include everything from our inner child, our procrastinator, our perfectionist and our free spirit, just to name a few. Each part makes up the whole package of our unique personality.

Think about the variety of thoughts that you have in a given day, and the parts of you that carry those thoughts towards fruition. How each part of your inner personalities drives you to move forward (or not) each day. Sometimes we feel utter joy in what we are doing and sometimes we are sad and miserable. Staying somewhat consistent is perhaps the key to finding our true Self or Selves. The human psyche and the variety of ticks that allows each of us to tock is really fascinating.

In my work as a business coach, I love watching people bring their dreams to life. I think that perhaps this is the most rewarding part of my work with entrepreneurs, as previously shared. Envisioning taking your life to exactly where you want it to be, followed up by the action of actually making it happen can bring us such great spiritual rewards.

Think about the variety of the people that you have met in your life, those who have made a profound impact and those who have just passed through your life. Undoubtedly those with a strong unique personality have affected your life the most. Their own life "glow" has allowed you to shine even brighter. Thus the reason it is critical to surround yourself with positive and inspiring people.

During the course of putting this book together, I have come to appreciate even more and comprehend on a deeper level the many teachings of Napoleon Hill, most especially his book, *Laws of Success*. It has been important to me to fully clarify and understand his thoughts and words. By doing so, I have become deeply inspired and in turn quite passionate about inspiring others on the principles as well.

It is amazing to me how many principles and ideas from over eighty years ago still hold true today. For example, take a read on his view of the Master Mind Principle of encompassing a pleasing personality:

"What is a Pleasing Personality? It is a personality that attracts, and in this lesson we will look at what causes that attraction and how to create it. Your personality is the sum total of your own characteristics and appearances that distinguish you from all others. The clothes you wear, the lines in your face, the tone of your voice, the thoughts you think, the character you have developed by those thoughts – all constitute parts of your personality. Whether your personality is attractive or not is another matter.

By far, the most important part of your personality is that part which is represented by your character. Therefore it is also the part that is not visible. The style of your clothes and their appropriateness undoubtedly constitutes a very important part of your personality, for it is true that people form first impressions of you from your outward appearance. Even the way you shake hands forms an important part of your personality and goes a long way toward attracting or repelling those with whom you shake hands. But this art can be cultivated."

What is probably most rewarding and inspiring about being truly your authentic self is that it is one of the main ingredients in fully participating in the law of attraction. True happiness is the essence of everything around you being in flow, starting from the inside and moving its way out.

The words of this chapter's Victory Letters will cover such topics as *Finding Your Truth* to *Lighting Your Fuse*. As you make your way to them I invite you to think about these words of Wilfred Peterson, an advertising executive who started writing for the magazine publication, *This Week,* in 1960. His column, *Words to Live By,* became so well read that it led to his highly popular book, *The Art of Living*. In his *Words to Live By* column in October 1961, he wrote these profound words:

"The art of being yourself, at your best, is the art of unfolding your personality into the person you want to be… Be gentle with yourself, learn to love yourself, to forgive yourself, for only as we have the right attitude toward ourselves can we have the right attitude toward others."

I invite you to fully appreciate all the gifts you bring as you turn the pages of the Victory Letters in this chapter. We will start out talking about the major role that love plays in who we are to ourselves as well as others. Focus on the varied personalities you possess as we further explore the **Master Mind Principle of Your Unique and Pleasing Personality.**

True Love

In love, as in martinis, feelings should be stirred, not shaken.
~Author Unknown

Happy Monday,

This is the week that contains the day in which we celebrate love. From paper valentines to yummy chocolates to sparkly things… yes, there are many ways to share our love for one another. However, perhaps the best thing to do is to stop and relish the love that has made our life what it is today.

From the love of our parents, which kept us feeling safe and warm, to that first crush that made us feel out of sorts and not sure what to do, love produces many feelings, some good, some not so good. I don't know about you, but I have cried many a tear over love.

In retrospect, the ups and downs of love have made each of us who we are today. Lost love, love won, love slipped away… true love found… all the components seem to work together.

In looking for a poem for today's letter I found one on the Internet entitled *True Love* by Helen Steiner Rice. (Author's Note: When I wrote to ask for permission to use this poem in the book her foundation said she did not write it. Therefore, the author of the beautiful poem I had shared in this Victory Letter is unknown, and I cannot share it with you here but invite you to go online and give it a read.)

The story of Helen Steiner Rice, which I had not known prior to finding this poem, is a compelling one full of how life can unfold for each of us in ways we had never expected. Helen was an amazing woman who came to find that she was a gifted writer who did not start her career in the 1920s with writing in mind. Yet she was so gifted at this craft that through the course of her career, she became quite renowned throughout the world. As her career progressed into the greeting cards industry, she found her love and passion, inspiring others with her words. She was given the title "Ambassador of Sunshine" by a colleague, which remains synonymous with her name today, over twenty years after her death. Many thanks to Helen for writing from her heart and to those who carry on her foundation to keep her work alive.

Who and what are the true loves and passions in your life today… right now? With whom can you celebrate love on February 14th, and perhaps the whole year through? The winter Olympics chose passion for the theme of this year's games, which is perhaps one of the strongest components of love. Yes, you would have to guess that many if not all of those athletes have a strong passion and love for what they do. You need to possess the strength of passion to get you through the ups and the downs… just like with any love.

So in the week ahead I wish you the opportunity to celebrate the many areas of your life where your heart finds love! Honor it and be thankful for it!

To Your Successes and Victories…

Your Power

Dwell in your possibilities.

~Emily Dickenson

Happy Monday,

On my desk are some post-it-notes with today's quote from Emily Dickinson on them. Over the past few days these words have been yelling out to me as I realize that I am indeed living amidst possibilities. The potential for my future exists as the world continues to speed forward, going round and round, bringing with it our life as it comes to be every day.

As the last couple of days have unfolded I have been reminded that no matter how we plan, life will in fact do what it does and give us things we don't necessarily want. Challenges, obstacles and situations come that are beyond our control, requiring us to add them into the mix of our lives.

For me, the first news of last week that I didn't want to hear is that a dear family friend had suffered a heart attack and slipped into a coma – a coma he would never wake from as he passed away on Thursday night from the world of those who loved him so dearly. His name was Cliff Prettyman and I can remember him from all the days of my life. He and his wife Mary Jo have been dear friends of my mom since she was in high school in Kansas City, Missouri.

The Prettymans migrated to Southern California as my parents did and while they lived an hour or more from us, their presence and friendship was always a part of our lives. As I became an adult I would see them every few years (not as often as I would have liked) and each time I did, it was always such a special treat. The one thing that crossed my mind when my mom let me know that Cliff had passed was the one single quality that outshone all his others.

That quality was how special Cliff made me feel whenever I was in his presence. I can especially remember the last time I saw him just a few short years ago. As he always did, he came and sat down, looked me straight in the eye and wanted to know what was happening in my life. He heard every word I said and as always, the conversation was full and rich. His presence, kindness and smile will be a part of me all the days of my life.

You just never know from day to day what the next moment may bring. Yesterday afternoon I found myself at the emergency room as I got the phone call from my husband that Bailey had had a bad fall while she was snowboarding at our local ski area. A frantic drive up the canyon, a fractured arm and an opposing sprained wrist left the day with nothing more than taking care of my daughter's needs, making sure she was as pain free as possible, feeling loved and cared for by her mother.

So fourteen days into this new year, I know there will continue to be challenges including many doctor visits over the next few days to deal with Bailey's pain. I will have my own appointments and commitments to reschedule as I restructure getting from Monday to Sunday again with new "to do's" in the mix of things.

But you know it's these challenges, these ups, downs, wins and deeply felt losses that make up the fibers of who we are. We can give up, cry a river, even say poor me, or we can take the lessons to be learned and continue moving forward towards our purpose(s), or sometimes even just move forward to find our purpose. We must continue to move, in order live the full life we were meant to have on this planet. We owe it to ourselves as well as those we love, those who have gone, and those who have yet to enter our lives.

What are your challenges in the week ahead? If you get tripped up along the way by the unknowns, what tools, methods or calming factors do you have at your fingertips that will get you back on track again? The key perhaps is the reminder to be in the moment with your possibilities, feel their ebb and flow and do what your heart, mind and spirit ask or need continuously from you.

Wishing you power and strength in your week ahead for you to be all that you can be, for yourself, as well as for those who love you and those who count on you to make a difference in their lives.

To Your Successes and Victories…

Valuing Relationships

Less is more.

~**Words of wisdom by someone**

Happy Monday,

The words of this week's quote repeated themselves to me time and time again over the course of this past week. Whether it was while writing or making recommendations to clients or being in situations with my kids – the words just kept ringing true.

Now this Monday morning as we shovel through another snowstorm (perhaps someone should get this message out to Mother Nature) the words continue to filter through my head.

One of my current reads is the book, *The Tipping Point, How Little Things Can Make a Big Difference,* by Malcolm Gladwell. During this past week while thinking about how less is more, ironically (or was it) one of the topics he covered in the book is the concept of less is more as it holds true in the relationships we keep, the relationships in both our personal and business lives. Sometimes when we try to take on more clients and friends, we find that we stop nurturing the ones we already have, the ones who already think we rock!

Who are the top 20 people in your personal life? According to *The Tipping Point*, when asked to write a list of people who you would be devastated by if they died, most people come up with 12. This, according to research, is because that is as much as your heart can hold. Who of your family and friends really holds your heartstrings?

Who are the top 20 or even the top 10 people in your business life? Think of those people who are always watching your back; those people who are perhaps mentors that get you excited about your work; those co-workers or colleagues that no matter what, you know you can count on as they help to make your work hum along each day; those clients who value who you are and the gifts you bring to them through your work.

My challenge to you in the week ahead is to remember who it is that you already have in your life. Make a list of those people that hit the top twenty of both lists. Think about how you can better value those relationships and make them stronger and even more meaningful.

Enjoy this week for exactly the gifts it brings to you!

To You Successes and Victories...

People Who Need People

The best thing to hold on to in life is each other.

~Audrey Hepburn

Happy Monday,

This Monday morning arrives reminding me that one of the greatest gifts we have in this life is indeed each other! During the past week I had several reminders of this. One of them included a visit from my mom for a couple of days, days that went by way too quickly and now leaves me missing her and looking forward to our next visit. I am trying to remember what she always likes to say: "Don't be sad our time together is over, be glad that it happened".

I was reminded also that most everyone who comes into our lives, even if for a brief few minutes, serves some kind of purpose for being there. Some give us inner strength, some give us love, some fascinate us, some we admire, some give us perspective, some annoy us, some make us angry, and some sadly… we are left wondering why our paths ever crossed at all.

Last Monday I was scheduled for jury duty so I drove through the snowstorm we were experiencing to get there and do my judicial duty. After worrying about being late, I waited for 1-1/2 hours before being called into the courtroom along with my fellow prospective jurors. Fortunately, I had the foresight to bring some paperwork along with me so I could accomplish something and not just end up staring at the people and the walls around me.

Upon leaving the jury room and getting into the courtroom, I found that it was enjoyable looking around at the others in the room as we each anxiously watched and listened to the judicial process. We were also all the while waiting to hear if the week before us would disappear into the Boulder Courthouse or if we could each get back to living our lives and earning a living. The first 13 were called and the cross examination began to see if they were "suitable" jurors. Being that I was not one of them, not only was there a feeling of relief, but it also gave me a great vantage point to watch the process. Those of us left had to hang around and wait in case any of the 13 was dismissed because of conflicting values, beliefs or "extenuating" circumstances.

Watching these people, my attraction to reality TV shows became more apparent. Yes, I do enjoy *The Apprentice, Survivor,* etc. and the people who are in them, people playing themselves. These jurors, who were complete strangers just a few minutes before, (remember I was too busy doing my paperwork to even look at them previously) started sharing their names, occupations, parent's occupations, marital status, children's information, books read, movies seen and of course their feelings on matters that pertained to the case at hand and beyond. Very interesting indeed, interest that turned into relief at the noon hour when I was able to head back into my own life as the jury was selected without me! Yeah!

People do make the world go round. We may not always agree with others or understand them, but they give us great insight and perspective if we choose to see. There are also people, who at the mere sight or mention of them can put a smile on our face. One thing I have come to realize for myself is my extreme shyness and self consciousness left me when I came to fully realize how much I liked other people and that meeting other people wasn't about me but about discovering them… what a great gift that can be in our lives!

So in the week ahead think about the people you come in contact with and how they impact your life. Stop and have a conversation with a stranger and see how it opens you up to new experiences. Pick up the phone and talk to someone you have not talked to in a long time. I have had that happen in a couple of instances lately and it has been wonderful. As Barbara Streisand sang…

"People, people who need people are the luckiest people in the world" (I sing this to my kids every once in a while just to make them crazy). Enjoy the week ahead and the people who come your way!

To Your Successes and Victories…

Happy Moments

The hours that make us happy make us wise.

~John Mansfield

Happy Monday,

Well, here it is Monday morning… I have officially gotten a year older; we have gone and come back from vacation; and now it is time for sports practices and getting ready for the school year ahead. Is there time this Monday morning to think about happiness and what it really means? To contemplate whether or not Mr. Mansfield was really correct in saying that happiness makes us wise? You probably know the answer because why else would I be writing to you…

Over the last couple of weeks I have had many snippets of happy moments enter my life. Ironically my sister gave me a book that I read from cover to cover while on vacation entitled, *Whatever Makes You Happy*. It's a fun, easy read novel about a woman in New York trying to find the meaning of happiness for a book she was writing. Turns out in the end that she had it all around her to begin with and she was looking for too much "theory" on the topic.

Happy moments really come in all different forms. While on vacation, probably one of the happiest moments I felt was the morning we picked up my son Travis from his two-week adventure with Outward Bound. There we were at the crack of dawn, our second day of vacation and we found ourselves in the beautiful little town of Marble, Colorado. We spent the night in a very "rustic" cabin as I tossed and turned all night, not sure if it was the rusticity of the cabin or the anticipation of seeing Travis in just a few short hours.

Well, finally and with much relief I got out of bed, got dressed, and then Ed, Bailey and I drove up to the end of the road where we were going to meet the group that Travis had been with for the last two weeks. Driving up this dirt road I had no idea what to expect but did know that my heart was missing my son a great deal. Never before had we been separated like this with no communication as he had spent the last two weeks roughing it in the great Colorado outdoors.

There, on this quiet mountain road, was a huge bus taking this group of teens back to Denver. All of a sudden people were everywhere, loading the bus with gear. As we pulled over, my eyes searched everywhere for Travis.

Then came the happy moment, the moment when, through the early morning light, Travis appeared at my window with a smile on his face that I will never forget. It was instantly obvious that my fifteen-year old son had grown up while away with this group of other teens and young adults. He looked more handsome than I could remember. My baby, my boy, was home and back with us, a new and changed young man. Happiness flooded every inch of my being as we hugged each other tightly.

Though these happy moments may not always make us wise (or do they?), they make us who we are and who we are going to be. They give us the reasons to get up this Monday morning and continue on our journey, when staying in bed might have been the easier way to go. And as I leave you this morning to go get my grown up son out the door for his first soccer practice of the season I know that my heart feels good and happy. I don't even mind getting another year older!

Wishing you happy moments in your week ahead!

To Your Successes and Victories…

Twists of Fate

Blame it on a simple twist of fate.
~Bob Dylan

Happy Monday,

This morning brings the first day of school! What a change from a week ago at this time when we were running to catch a boat to Catalina. With the kids out the door and gone to school, I can feel their absence shift the energy in the house. Part of me is excited with the extra time I will have to work my business and part of me misses them already, feeling a bit of melancholy sadness of summer coming to a close.

We did have a fabulous trip over the past two weeks that ended our summer break with a bang! As we traveled home, the miles between California and Colorado allowed my mind to wander through the special times our summer brought to us. Ironically, or perhaps in confirmation, as we pulled onto our street after 15 hours on the road, Bob Dylan sang the words of this week's quote, "A Simple Twist of Fate." It had been something I was thinking about during the drive, how fate plays a role in so much of what happens in our life, the people we meet and the happenings of our lives.

The wedding and the events surrounding our trip to California were beautiful and wonderful. The bride and groom, Gretchen and Toby, made the ultimate life commitment after knowing each other since their early teens. At the age of 13 or so, they met each other through a family member and began sharing occasional family events together. Nothing romantic happened though they always thought of each other as "special" people. That was until a simple email brought them together in their adult life about two years ago. They took fate one-step further and found they held a deep love for each other. Indeed, a twist of fate.

The friends I spent time with in California are ones you have heard me speak of often in my letters – Nancy (Gretchen's mother) and Linda. I think one of the greatest gifts my parents ever gave me was sending me to Our Lady of Lourdes School in Tujunga, California. Not necessarily for the education (though I probably learned more in the eight years spent there than in the subsequent four years in pubic school) but for the blessing of life long friendships formed in the first grade with these two girls.

Even though we now all live in different parts of the country, our friendship remains strong. We even had the chance to connect with our childhood friends Cathy and Susan. It is amazing how the time and distance always seem to fade away when we are all together – another twist of fate.

The development of my relationship with my husband, Ed, still amazes me at times, even after 21 years of marriage. In our mid-twenties we became next-door neighbors, never really giving each other a second look beyond that of a very mild friendship. Over the course of a couple of years, both of our marriages self-destructed and we both became single once again. Then one fate-filled day we looked at each other and realized that an attraction existed we had never felt before. Yes, another twist of fate.

I could share many other examples in my life as you could share about yours. We can do all the planning in the world – but fate does play a role that spices up the playing field a bit. Perhaps the key here is to think of what our life would be like had we not acted on the gifts fate has presented to us. In my teenage years when Linda and Nancy and I moved away from each other we had the choice to not stay in contact. But we did. I could have ignored my change of feelings for Ed, just as Gretchen could have with Toby, but we didn't. When the time was right, we knew that it was time to move forward… together.

Fate places people and situations into our life, and what we choose to do with them makes our life what it is. Sadly, fate also takes people away from our life through deaths and broken relationships. The ebb and flow, I suppose. There is a saying and belief that "everything happens for a reason." We just need to be fully aware enough to pay attention when it does.

As you look ahead into your week, think about the twists of fate you have reacted to and those that you did not – we all have them.

What fate in front of you right now will you choose to take or leave? What twist of fate have you not thought of or been grateful for in a long while?

Open your heart and mind to those things you have been given along your way, think of them perhaps as your fates of victory!

Wishing you a week full of watching your life with your eyes wide open!

To Your Successes and Victories…

Essence of a Legacy

One life can make such an impact.
Each life has the potential to leave a lasting legacy.
~Gwen Lavenue

Happy Monday,

Happy Christmas Eve! A calm always settles in with Christmas less than 24 hours away. No matter how much there is left to do, there has always been a certain peace I have felt every Christmas Eve since I was a child.

The cards and letters have been streaming in from family and friends, as always, and it has been great to hear the news and see the pictures of those we care about. The other day a card arrived that really has been the most meaningful for me in "feeling" the essence of this season. It came from a friend, Gwen Lavenue, and the words she made, really touched my heart and soul.

Those words – used in the quote of today's letter – about one life having an impact, in memory of her mother whom she lost this year, really hit me. So as I am prone to do, and yes it makes my family a bit crazy sometimes, I thought about how I could incorporate this thought into our Christmas dinner. Now understand that I am feeling incredibly blessed to have my mother at the table with us this year, as there were many possibilities that it was not going to happen.

So I asked my mom to write our names on the bookmarks I planned to use for place cards in her special writing that we all know and love. Then I asked her to write one word on the back of the bookmark that would describe a quality about that family member.

The idea is that at Christmas dinner as my mom shares with us some special words of love, she will light her candle and from her candle, light the candle of the person next to her. Each person then in turn will light the candle of the person next to them sharing their special word that appears on the back of each bookmark.

The hope is that by the time we make it around our table of 16, we will have illuminated more than the table itself. We will have shared how each of us makes a difference in our family.

Enjoy your time together with those you love and care about in the days ahead. Remember that families aren't perfect, but if you can remember even that single quality that makes each person unique – it will make it the holiday full of the love and sharing that it is meant to have.

I wish you a wonderful Christmas! May the peace and love of today and tomorrow carry you throughout the year ahead.

To Your Successes and Victories…

Getting out of Line

In order to be irreplaceable one must always be different.

~Coco Chanel

Happy Monday,

I write to you this morning with the light of day barely breaking through the clouds. It is amazing how dark the mornings have become – makes it a wee bit harder to get up when it is still dark outside. It's also a sure sign that daylight savings is in our near future. In fact, many signs are all around us right now as the season continues to change.

Yesterday afternoon, with thoughts of living in the present really vibrating through my head, I had a nice time of "being", hanging out in my kitchen making salsa from an abundant crop of tomatoes that keeps producing, looking out as the rain washed over the beautiful ash tree outside my kitchen window ablaze in yellows and gold's, spending time with my family, making a pot of chicken and dumplings, all topped off with watching the Rockies win yet another game last night – inching closer to winning the pennant and heading into the world series! Amazing! I couldn't have planned a more perfect Sunday afternoon and evening.

During these days of Fall, perhaps more than any other time of year, it seems as though Mother Nature has given us a fabulous reminder of the importance of living in the moment. The trees and bushes are alive with burning colors that will oh so quickly be gone. It's a treat to go anywhere right now and see the changing landscape. Trees that you may have barely noticed before all of sudden stand out from the rest because of their blazing glory.

This of course brings us to this week's quote from Coco Chanel, a woman who took the world of fashion by storm, especially in the 50s and 60s. The art of standing out from the crowd by letting your own unique self come into bloom is perhaps the greatest gift we can give ourselves, letting those special qualities that lay inside of us emerge as we share them with the world.

It surprises me at times when I see how, as people, we can fall into a "sleep" pattern with our lives. Not too long ago, I had a conversation with a coach and facilitator on the Victory Circles team, who shared with me a story about a visit to a cheese factory. She noted how she took a tour through this factory in Oregon, and at the end of the tour there was a long line for something. Not sure what they were doing, she headed to the front of the line to discover that all these people were waiting in line for a tiny cheese sample. Following the crowd and doing what they were doing, for such a small reward, was not something she opted to do.

How about you? How often do you get out of the line and create your own path, with no one in front of you to delay your journey, make you wait or stop you completely? There is something I love about breaking free from a pack of cars on the highway and having no one in front of me to slow me down! Perhaps it's one of the things I love about rising early in the morning – you can find yourself with time that no one has yet touched – a place in time to call your own!

In the week ahead I wish you the time, space and energy to enjoy the world around you as you make your own special way on your amazing journey!

To Your Successes and Victories…

CHAPTER 7

Victory...
And Accurate Thinking

Finding Clarity in
Your Thoughts, Decisions and Beliefs

Inside me where no one else goes,

I see what no one else can see.

It keeps me focused through the storms,

Joyous in my victories!

The human brain is believed to have the capacity to orchestrate, on average, 65,000 thoughts during the course of an 18-hour day. That equates to basically a thought per second. This activity, a lot like breathing, can be something we tend to take for granted. While thoughts happen automatically it doesn't necessarily mean we are in fact fully activating our ability to think. Consider someone sitting in front of a TV set or doing any kind of activity that puts his or her brain into autopilot just absorbing the thoughts of others.

Thinking is defined as "using the mind to reason or reflect – using the mind to form unique thoughts." So here is the burning question… of your 65,000 thoughts you have each day, how many are truly unique to you? How often do you give yourself the time and space to really, really put your thinking skills into action in order to make a difference in your business and/or your life?

Visualization is a different type of thinking; it is creative more than analytical. Visualizing allows you to "paint" your dreams. Dreaming gives us hope and belief in what we are able to manifest through the power of our thinking. It can be a marvelous cycle: Thinking – Visualizing – Dreaming – Hoping – Thinking. This process is the ideal of why it is so important to actively work our thinking muscles as opposed to passively processing our thoughts.

Stop and (yes), think, about how much you get accomplished in your head when you give yourself the time and opportunity to do so. Life just seems to click along better when we can move without stress and anxiety blocking our thinking path. In day-to-day living it can become difficult to feel the peace required to put one unique thought after another. Without putting in "thinking time" it usually only happens haphazardly.

The key factor is getting rid of the noise that can start to build up around us. Noise comes in many forms, from the news media rattling off the latest negative information of the day, to constantly living by a "to do list." Suddenly you are just *doing* instead of *being*. I have found that this can create a blockage sometimes that leads to the stress, frustration and ultimate burnout.

Our emotions play a strong role in the peace we feel inside. Whether happiness and joy, sorrow and grief, our emotions all are part of the make-up of what we feel. Isn't it better to feel something as opposed to nothing at all?

Recently, I have taken on a whole new appreciation for something that we have the ability to during these moments of every day... again, something as basic as breathing. When we get stressed, our breathing becomes very shallow and weak. When this occurs we can tend to forget the adage, "out with the old and in with the new". Taking just short choppy breaths is really not good for our overall health. As you read this now, stop and take a really deep breath from your gut, belly and chest. Spend a couple minutes doing this and see how much better you feel! A miraculous result is available to us just for the asking – or breathing!

Breathing is an important component of meditation because it allows you to get into your core and let your inner body connect with your brain. It can give you clarity and peace as well as increase your ability for much clearer thinking.

About a year ago I was given a few meditative exercises to do that helped me to sleep like a baby. Doing them as I got into bed at night helped me to fall into a deep and extremely restful sleep. I encourage you to try it too. Simply close your eyes and envision yourself in front of a staircase – the staircase can be of any design that you choose. This is where I had fun, creating different architectural renderings of staircases from classic to modern. You want to envision yourself climbing those stairs one by one, counting out the 50 stairs that it is going to take you to get to the top.

Take your time; enjoy what you see along the way whether it is perhaps pictures on the stairwell wall or a beautiful view from large glass windows. Open your mind – let it be.

When I started doing this exercise I would fall asleep before I even got to the top of the first flight, getting so immersed in the details of the climb. As I did it more, I finally did make it to the top of the staircase. What was before me was a long hallway, just as it should be for you. Here is where you want to walk down the hallway seeing many different doors along the way. Let your mind again open up and try to envision the different colors and textures of the doors and the hallway.

Of the doors you see, you want to choose one to walk through. Watch yourself putting your hand on the knob, turning it, and opening the door. What is on the other side of the door? What is in the room? It can be anything your mind chooses it to be. Last year when I opened the door for the first time I was delighted to find that I had entered a tropical hut that was wide open a beautiful blue-green ocean on the opposite side of the room. The colors and feeling of being in the tropics were so distinct that I could even hear that sound water makes when it is just barely moves in a gentle summer breeze.

There on the other end of the room right before the drop off into the ocean was a beautifully handcrafted wicker-style desk and ornate chair just waiting for me. Waiting for me to sit at it and write, to write and write some more to my heart's content. What a delicious sight this was for to me, one that has stayed in my mind – bringing me peace whenever I think of it. In this meditation, the journey to get to the top of the stairs and into my beautiful tropical room took me about three weeks. I was about to give up on getting through any of the doors in the hallway and when I finally did, I was able to unlock my deepest desire – to write without a care in the world.

What are your desires? The inner parts of you have been waiting to come out and play with the rest of you. Sometimes it is about just finding that stillness that we get when we are fully rested and able to think things through. Imagine it this way, the difference between calm water and water that is choppy and creating large waves. The difference in the calm water is that you can see clearly all the way to the bottom. Every detail from the plant life under the surface to the multitude of fish that may be swimming around becomes clear to the eye.

Finding clarity in our thinking can bring us a great deal of inner peace. If the water is calm you can actually see your reflection. With choppy, turbulent water – your reflection disappears. I encourage you to find your path to the water's edge, taking the steps that you need to take to allow you to discover more about yourself.

Author and motivational speaker Brian Tracy laid out the aspect of thinking in this light…

"All improvement in your life begins with an improvement in your mental pictures. Your mental pictures act as a guidance mechanism that causes you to act in ways that make your mental pictures come true in your life."

As you read and hopefully fully absorb into your mind the Victory Letters in this chapter it is my hope that you full open up and become even more aware of the power in your minds eye. Get the full capacity of your brain working as you learn to appreciate the *Master Mind Principle of Accurate Thinking.*

Thinking it Through

Thinking is the hardest work there is,
which is probably the reason why so few engage in it.
~Henry Ford

Happy Monday,

How much time per day do you spend thinking? I don't mean just having thoughts cruising through your head but really do what has been termed as *critically thinking*? It's amazing in this era we now live in, that we spend so much time having other peoples thoughts – whether in the emails we get, the TV programs we watch, the information we read… thoughts of others are constantly passed our way. The question is, what do we do with them?

This past week I had an interesting experience that got me thinking about this subject. It was over something as small as a pothole. Over the last few months, every time I head into the parking lot of my grocery store I have encountered several potholes. Seemingly strategically placed to annoy, they are pretty hard to avoid either on the way in or the way out, especially the bigger they continue to get.

Each time I drive over these potholes with other "thoughts" already going through my head I am annoyed because of the jarring motion as well as the fact that they are going to do some damage to my car one of these days. But what happens is that by the time I get to the check-out line at the store with hundreds of other thoughts going through my head (meal planning, next errand to run, clients to call, etc.) I have forgotten to say anything to the grocery store manager.

Eureka! Last Thursday I remembered and I mentioned it to the cashier while she was checking me out. She instantly started talking about the pothole saying it had been bugging her also but she didn't know what was going on with it. She called the store manager over who began with, "Oh the pothole, I would love to tell you about the pothole…" and he did. Suddenly everyone around me was talking about the pothole, saying they had been meaning to talk to someone about it. (Turns out the store manager had been trying to do something about it for months but had to deal with a lot of corporate red tape in order to rectify the problem.)

The point here is we all have thoughts. The difference comes when take them out of our head and put them into action. Without that piece of implementation we never get the opportunity to share them with others and they fade away in our brains.

What if we spent the week ahead thinking things all the way through? You know, that thought that came up about a business you wanted to start, a new direction you wanted to take in your business, that proposal you wanted to give your boss on a new way to manage work flow, a vacation you wanted to take… the list goes on and on. Obviously to think each of these ideas through requires that commodity we have so little of – time. So focus on the ideas that never fully came to life because of time holding you back. If you were to push through and find the time I think you would begin to amaze yourself at the level of new accomplishments in your life.

Sometimes it can be scary to think something through from just a fleeting thought to a full-blown idea that is put into action. *Especially* if it is a good enough idea that we know we must move forward quickly before someone else takes our idea and brings it to life for themselves.

So in the week ahead, I offer you more than a penny for your thoughts… I offer you the idea of bringing your thoughts to the point of something solid and tangible, giving yourself and your thoughts the time you deserve. Hopefully, the result is that you act upon something you have wanted to do for some time. Remember, each of us really can make a difference.

To Your Successes and Victories…

Adventure around the Corner

Life is like school. You have to pass one test to get on to the next test.

~Betty Morgan

Happy Monday,

Don't know about you but some days I feel like there are way too many tests in life. You know, those little life lessons that make you go, "Oh yeah, right, that is what I was supposed to do." This past week as my kids headed off to school (Trav started high school!), it was a reminder that they have so many lessons still ahead of them, and as much as I would like to help them along their way, they will have to learn most of them at this point on their own. My role will be to try and guide them as I can (and as they will listen) and to have the band-aids ready just as I did when they were little.

If we think back to the biggest "aha" moments we have had in our lives they usually came after suffering a failure or an upset of one kind or another. For example, those moments spent as a teen staring at your ceiling feeling like the most crucified kid in the world after suffering a parental grounding for going out of bounds and breaking the rules. Now, of course, I look back and am thankful that my parents slowed me down (a bit) by doing that, but in reality I was on a roll of living my life that they could not stop. I was carefree and looking for adventure around every corner.

Thinking about it now part of me misses that girl I used to be and I do think it is better to live life looking for the lessons to be learned as opposed to always having the answers. Answers are good but not always as much fun. Of course having some of the answers is also good. Perhaps as with everything in life it's about finding balance between lessons to learn and knowing the road you are traveling on.

As I watched the closing ceremonies last night, it was hard for me not to think about lessons learned by those athletes who did not win the gold during the Olympics. Yes, the glory does go to those who win the gold, but the stories yet to be told are of those who came so close and learned lessons that perhaps will take them to Beijing – or perhaps just on with their lives, lives that will be different because of the experiences they had over the past few weeks.

So in the week ahead, what if you looked at the lessons you have learned in life, both big and small, and how they have changed you as a person, how they have made you the person you are right now today and who you might be tomorrow. They can be big, like discovering what really makes your heart sing and they can be small like how to make a good pasta dinner (though some might think that's pretty big also!).

The key for me anyway is continuing to test my strengths and my abilities to make sure I am getting the most out of what I was given to create on this planet. This is my opportunity… my one go around to make it happen. You know, I guess that is why it is so great to talk to those who have traversed the road before us and see where their tests have left them in their hearts and their souls.

Remember, we can't always study from a book what lessons we need to learn… just living life can be the best way to really bring clarity to lessons. Sometimes deepening our convictions to stay the course and sometimes changing the course completely.

I hope this week that you are able to move out of your comfort zone and test yourself… learning and growing as you go! Because in the end, while the test itself and the "grade" you receive may be a painful… you may be amazed by what you find… especially because you are the one who really grades it. Have Fun.

To Your Successes and Victories…

A Different Light

Sometimes I do get to places just when God's ready
to have somebody click the shutter.
~Ansel Adams

Happy Monday,

As the pinks of the morning sky signal a new day it is time to begin a new week in our lives. I hope this Monday morning finds you well and ready to begin new adventures. This is our last week of evening light as daylight savings begins next Saturday night. It is a good time to enjoy the full light of each of the next six days.

Light… it is interesting to think about how we see things differently because of the light shed on an idea, a thought or a physical object. One afternoon last week while walking my pooch, Sam, I was stopped in my tracks before getting to the lake at the end of our street. I stopped because I was so touched by the way the sunlight reflected on the valley that lies before our great Rocky Mountains. Having walked this road hundreds of times in the twelve years we have lived on this street, it was intriguing to realize that I had never before seen the light just this way.

There was Haystack Mountain, which is a little cone-looking hill that just rises up out of the Boulder valley. Next to it is an amazing mesa that I had just never noticed before. The way the light from the sun through the clouds was now shining on the mesa brought it to life for me. It was beautiful. Sure, I have driven past the mesa zillions of times but to see it in this particular way was beautiful and I felt very blessed to be standing there in that moment. As the course of the week went by, perhaps because of the changing of the season, I continued to see things "in a new light".

Now the question is, was it because I was taking the time to look or was it because there was something new to see? In thinking about writing about light this morning it came to me that of course good photographers are the masters of light. They know how to play with it just right to get the look they are hoping to achieve. Sometimes discovery and experimentation process make all the difference.

Ansel Adams was a genius at this and the most remarkable thing is his most beloved work was done without depending on studio lights. He photographed by the light of the sun or the lack thereof. At the age of 14, he became quite intrigued by the power of the camera and it became his life's work. The quote in this week's letter as well as looking at his photography is a great depiction of just that idea of how we sometimes end up in the right place at the right time and are able to snap a picture, at least in our mind, of the beauty around us.

Sadly though, we tend to get so wrapped up in the running around of life that we miss these moments given to us for free. By being unable to stop and enjoy what "is," we can tend to get focused on the "have to get done or become," and simply put, we can lose out on so much. Perhaps my seeing those beautiful images in my world this past week was a special gift given when my awareness shifted. With Ed was off working in France (catching his own special lights… I'm sure) and my plate being way too full I couldn't have seen anything frankly without that shift. Truth is those moments really helped me to stop and catch my breath.

What are some special moments of light waiting for you this week? Take that walk you have been meaning to take, fully watch the sunrise or sunset and appreciate the beauty in it. Guaranteed, the 15–20 minutes you take will be well worth it. Feeling stressed or, overwhelmed? What better way to remove those worries than to look at something really beautiful… and to feel the true essence of it's light?

I wish you a great week of beauty and grace as you see things in a new light!

To Your Successes and Victories…

Dreaming

Yesterdays over my shoulder so I can't look back for too long, there's just too much at sea waiting in front of me and I know that I just can't go wrong.

~Jimmy Buffett

Happy Monday,

OK… here we are, it's Monday morning and imagine this… instead of sitting at your desk reading this e-mail you are cruising along the ocean on a beautiful blue-sky day, not a care in the world as you let your mind just float along not really thinking or doing… just being, as the rays of the sun provide your motivation for the day.

Ahh… sound good? It does to me, too! What if you could just hold on to the thought and the feel of the sunshine and have it carry you through your day? Indeed, that is what having a goal, a plan, and a dream can do for us sometimes. It keeps us sailing along.

What are your dreams? What is it that gets you excited when you start to think about it? What is it that captures the essence of you? Can you make a career out of it or build your career around it?

Last week I had the opportunity to hear a number of successful people talking about how they created success in their life and how it has allowed for more blue-sky days than they ever thought possible. Not at 65 but now, today (one woman was in her early 40s). The common theme was planning – planning for a future that insured a more enjoyable today and the ability to spend their lives with those they loved.

As I began to think about planning (it ultimately became the theme of the week last week), I was compelled to take pen to paper and review some of my plans for my business and my life. My business has been changing a great deal over the past seven months and I realized that I had been just letting it happen. What I found, as I usually do, is that plans take on a whole different look and feel when you put them down on paper. It is the commitment to have a written plan that makes you just that committed to making it happen.

As I worked on my planning I heard the song from Jimmy Buffett ("Changes in Latitudes, Changes in Attitudes") and realized that while we need to look back at our mistakes in order to move forward, we cannot look back for too long. The other aspect is there are so many options in front of us that if we don't make choices we can just find ourselves overwhelmed by it all and end up sitting still in the water with no wind to move our sails.

So as you set sails this week, how about thinking about your plan of action for the life you want to be living? When was the last time you wrote down a plan of action that would allow you to reach your dreams – your sunshine? Find a place that you enjoy being, a place where you can hear yourself think. Give yourself at least one hour (two would be great, three terrific) and answer these questions:

1. Where do you want to be in 3 months, 6 months, one year and five?

2. How are you going to get there?

3. What is the main vehicle that will take you there?

4. How will you enjoy the ride along the way?

5. Who are the key people you want with you on this journey?

6. What distractions, annoyances and negatives do you need to eliminate?

7. How can you financially support your plans?

8. What talents do you possess that are going to get you where you want to go?

9. Who or what has been stopping you?

10. What is at least one thing you can do everyday to ensure this plan will work?

Have fun and be creative in this process. First write from the heart and then fine tune from there. Surround yourself with people who inspire you and then go for it! Anything is possible if first you believe. Have a great week and feel the sunshine!

To Your Successes and Victories...

Forming Thoughts

When a person dies, a library burns.

~Alex Haley

Happy Monday,

This week's quotation is one of my favorites. When was the last time you wrote down your thoughts? Yes, those constant little words you have consciously and subconsciously wheeling through your brain on a consistent basis.

The term "journaling" has been used for capturing your thoughts onto paper or the computer. You could call the Victory Letters a form of journaling, as they are thoughts of mine that I share with you each week. These letters have become more than I originally thought they would be when I started writing them.

Little did I know what was to unfold for me that first Monday morning when I sat down to share some positive words as I looked for the daily victories in my own life. What I found was that thoughts in my head took on a life of their own when they became written words. Of course, I would have never imagined that this practice would allow for a dream of mine to come true… to write my first book.

The truth is that I was afraid to write, afraid that I would not put the perfect words down on paper. A few classes at CU many years ago left me very intimidated and thinking that everything I wrote had to be perfectly structured. What ended up happening was once I made the commitment to write, forgetting about the structure, the thoughts were able to easily escape.

I found with the Victory Letters that the more I wrote the more the thoughts started flowing. Just as our brain is constantly flowing so can the words we think flow onto paper. As you may have noticed, my letters to you are not always perfect (thank goodness for the team of editors on my first book) but I have gotten much better, and of course spell check is a friend I would not be without.

The fact of the matter is this: There are words and thoughts and connections in our brain that when it shuts down during our final moments on this planet we will never be able to share again. The words we have right now, today, are a piece of us that could make a difference for future generations, even if it is in only for our own families. What if our written words made a difference while we are still around to enjoy them?

Words are a treasure. We use them everyday. What if you took the time to really express the thoughts in your head in a clear concise way? We most often use the verbal form of words as our daily communication – even though email has brought writing back to us in a different form.

Just as words emerge as we talk, the same can happen when you get into the flow of writing. Letting your subconscious mind allow words to escape from you in the written form is pretty incredible if you just let it happen.

I feel extremely blessed to have the ability to write. Was I born with it? I am not so sure. In fact, I had a few teachers along the way who had their doubts about me. I think it took just doing it consistently that allowed the process to happen for me, just taking it in small little doses so I did not feel overwhelmed in letting my creative side come out. Now, if anything, I have something to leave my children so they can know some of the thoughts I experienced in my life.

So as you move through your week, think about what it is you have to share. I love what Carl Jung had to say… "But if you have nothing at all to create, then perhaps you create yourself." Have a great week enjoying your ability to form thoughts through the power of the written word.

To Your Successes and Victories…

The Silent Spot

The quieter you become the more you are able to hear.

~Zen Wisdom

Happy Monday,

As the engines of your week begin to turn and the noise of activities takes you away into your week… I hope you can remember a recent silent moment that will carry you through the week ahead. Silence, it's that moment in time when we don't hear any noise from the inside out. Just the blanket of stillness… it can be very refreshing and very nourishing to our spirits.

This past Saturday gave us a beautiful night with the Harvest Moon shining brightly. After returning home from a party, Ed and I sat out in our back yard enjoying a fire in our fire pit. While sitting there enjoying the quiet with just the occasional popping of the fire and light conversation, I was drawn to my garden which was almost as light as day from the brightness of the moon. The blanket of silence filling the space gave magic to the garden… as if I could almost hear the garden fairies flying around it was so silent. Truly, it was a moment in time that I won't soon forget.

Each day we have so much coming at us. Add to that the noise from TV, the Internet, radio, etc., and it can be overwhelming. It is amazing that something so simple as complete silence can be such a challenge for many of us. What if we tried to incorporate silence into our daily life, to find that silent spot within us that really makes us complete? I would suppose for many of us that prayer and meditation are great enhancers of the gift of silence. So as you move about your week… listen for the silent moments and let them strengthen you, and help you get into your groove, finding the real essence of you. Silence indeed can be golden!

To Your Successes and Victories…

Heart Butterflies

In order to succeed we must first believe that we can.

~Michael Korda

Happy Monday,

Easter Monday has arrived, leaving Easter a happy memory. On Saturday I decided to feel the essence of Easter by going to see *The Passion of the Christ*. While I had been putting it off because of the emotion and violence in it, I knew the time had come for me to witness it for myself. Indeed, it impacted me deeply and left me with many emotions.

Having grown up Catholic and learning this story over and over again I never felt the sadness so deeply as I did in watching this movie. One of the things I walked away thinking a great deal about was the power of belief. No matter your religious orientation, belief is a powerful thing to possess in your spirit, whether it is the belief in your faith or in the aspirations for your life. Many great things have been accomplished in our world due to this power.

The important thing I feel is to believe in something and have it touch you in your heart as well as your soul. For me, I will never forget the first time I felt what I have come to call "spirit," right smack dab in the middle of my heart and my soul. Keep in mind that I have been a recovering Catholic for most of my adult life, never quite sure where it fits in with my personal beliefs.

It happened one weekend when Ed, the kids and I took a trip down to southern Colorado to visit the Great Sand Dunes National Park and the surrounding area. We ended up by accident in a little town called San Luis, a quaint town that is one of the oldest in Colorado (founded in 1851). We decided to visit the Stations of the Cross, the Catholic symbolism for Christ's final days on earth, on the hill overlooking this beautiful farming community.

At the end of the stations was a beautiful little chapel that only added to something that I found growing in my heart that afternoon. As I walked out of the chapel and stood in the sunshine overlooking the valley below, it hit like a butterfly in my heart: I felt a spiritual presence in my life like I never have felt before… the true essence of the power of belief for probably the first time in my whole life. It had a profound effect on me.

Belief is powerful. It is an emotion that can drive people to do great things with their lives. Just as author Michael Korda says in the quote here in today's letter, belief allows us to succeed in our life. Everyone hits obstacles along the way and if you don't really believe in what you are doing you find yourself stopping in your tracks and sometimes even back peddling.

Think about the times you have been excited or energized about a project before you, and something happens that you had not anticipated. What did you do? Did you stop altogether or did you recharge and keep going? What did it cost you to stop or to find the strength to head in a new direction?

This week I would love for you to think about what it is that helps you to believe. If you have lost your belief in yourself, what is it that is keeping you from true happiness? What steps can you do to find it? If there is one thing I believe in strongly, that is again the ultimate power of the human spirit.

Wishing you a full and powerful week ahead!

To Your Successes and Victories…

Finding New Ways

Curiosity is the key to creativity.

~Akio Morita

Happy Monday,

As today starts, how curious are you about the week that is about to unfold in front of you? Think of it. You could look at it as 7 days or 168 hours or even 10,080 minutes. They are all yours, to do with, as you will.

This is the beginning of your week. Yes, you have to share it with a few million other people on the planet but the time in front of you is yours and no one else's. You could look at the things you need to accomplish as drudgery or you can look at them as possibilities for creative energy.

Last week I wrote to you about innovation, and to innovate you need curiosity. Yes, the curiosity to create something that was not there before, to bring something to life or to make something that was there work even better.

Just imagine how curious Thomas Edison must have been to harness the electricity that Benjamin Franklin had discovered. It kept him trying over and over and over again until he got it right. What was in the power that pushed Madame Curie to such profound discovery that she become the first woman to earn a Nobel Prize and then the first person to ever win two of them?

Sure you might think, all that could be done has been done. Those who came before us already did it all. Or you might think that you are too busy with what "has" to get done to be curious about what could be done. But I want to challenge you this week to think differently, to get out of your "normal" mode, and see beyond the norm toward what's possible.

Your new idea could be to create a bigger fundraiser than your kid's school has ever seen before or maybe a an effective new system that could save your company time and money. Create an improved way to get from here to there by finding a new shortcut. Even if it is finding a new driving short cut home that saves you time.

You could find a new way to wear your hair or go shopping for a look you have not tried before. How about that website you have been meaning to create, the writing you might like to get done, a new recipe to delight your taste buds (and those around you!), planting a new kind of seed you have never tried before as the earth around us begins to wake up from winter? What about taking a ride down a road that you have always been curious about? Your limits are only what you decide to let them be.

Perhaps you have the opportunity to think something new. Anatole France, another Nobel Prize winner, thought of learning in this light: "The whole art of teaching is only the art of awakening the natural curiosity of young minds for the purpose of satisfying it afterwards." Remember, we are as young in spirit as we choose to let ourselves be. Discovering the gifts that others bring into our lives is also another way to uncover new things in our world.

In the week ahead I wish you the time and space to let your curiosity bring you gifts you can't even imagine at this moment.

To Your Successes and Victories…

CHAPTER 8

Victory...
And the Power
of Concentration

Focus and Attention to the Details

Right in front of me is the opportunity
To put into action,
What I can clearly see,
Filling my senses and being,
With light and clarity.

Let's face it… we have a lot of stuff coming at us on a very regular basis. The only way we seem to be able to stop it from coming at us is to go on vacation. And even then, if we are not careful… we can still have it coming at us. The stuff coming at us in this age of information technology can actually stop us from gaining success in life. With too much swirling around us it makes it very difficult to focus and ultimately concentrate on what we are doing.

There is a strong connection between focus and success. Simply look at any successful athlete who has become a champion at the sport he or she participates in. The athlete's success is due to many factors, but most notably two skills they have in abundance which are focus and concentration. These skills insure that they train religiously, and come game day, the champions have nothing but the game on their minds. Think about the times you give whatever you are doing 100% of your focus and how much you get accomplished.

The vacation overdrive syndrome is a time when most people can achieve miraculous feats in just a matter of days. I bet you know that adrenaline rush you get days before going on vacation. In order to get out the door and then fully relax when you do requires actually getting everything done so you can go play. Could it be your passion for going on vacation that gets you going? I think it must be so.

Each of us brings our own unique passion to the things we love to do. Think about when you are in the "zone" of your peak concentration levels. There you are humming along, losing all touch with the time and events that move past you in the process. You are concentrating because you *want* to concentrate. Now don't get me wrong, shit happens. In fact, as I write these words today I have had a number of interruptions, from the teenagers in my world to our new puppy gallivanting all around me. My triple role this morning as Mother, Author and Entrepreneur kicked in and I had to insure the house did not burn down, literally. I just had to remember to continue to pull back to what I really needed to get done today and that was to write this chapter.

Let's address some questions I often hear on this topic when we utilize this principle in the Victory Circles. The question often is, "What happens when I want to do something I am passionate about and can't seem to concentrate on it because of too much chaos around me?" The easiest answer to that scenario, which may seem way to simplistic, is either get rid of or get out of the chaos. Find and embrace a place that you can call your own without day-to-day interruptions. A place where you can concentrate on what is important to you at a given time. Sometimes this "place" can in fact be the time of day. I find when I start my morning at 5 am I'm amazed by the feats I can accomplish before the household and world wake up at 7am. That's two glorious hours all to me! Other people I know find the midnight hour to be a great time to really focus.

Why wait until your back is against the wall to really and fully concentrate on items in your business and life that pull on your passion strings? Could the answer be that you are spending too much time looking at the wrong things? Has someone (perhaps even you) given you doubt or worry that your passion is not what it should be?

My clients and I have all experienced the dreaded "guilt" factor. That inner inkling that no matter what you do, you feel like you should be doing something else. If you are focused on your business and not the family for instance you feel family negligence guilt, and vice versa, business guilt when spending time with the family.

The key is finding that proverbial balance – yes, I hate to say it but it is true. If you have multiple things that are pulling at your attention, you must find a way to create a life that does not have the scales tipping too much one way or the other.

For many entrepreneurs, that which we love can become our curse. Our passion becomes our business and then if we don't manage it properly it can become our nemesis. The key, as any truly successful entrepreneur will tell you, is the knowing what tasks you do well and then letting others take care of what you don't do so well. By ensuring that all the details of the business have been taken care of, you are then able to focus on and enjoy why you started the business in the first place, to do what you are really good at doing.

A must-read if you are in business for yourself is the *E-myth Revisited* by Michael Gerber. I myself like to freshen up on it about once a year because of its tried and true methods that that show the reader how to concentrate on what we want to do most. These methods are put into systems that work in getting us to think through processes that help us fully concentrate. While the book is focused on business – it is in fact something that is possible to incorporate into the many aspects of our lives.

So how do you live with all your passion engaged? What are the gifts that you can give to yourself when you have fallen and it feels like gravity is holding you tightly down? Many things contribute to belief and they include but are not limited to:

ATTITUDE – The power of positive thinking

LOVE – Filling your life with people and things you can and want to embrace.

FAITH – Belief in that which you cannot see except for in your mind's eye.

EMPOWERMENT – Giving yourself the ability to move mountains as you gain the knowledge and resources that are abundantly available to you.

DELEGATION – How many things are you currently doing yourself that you could and should give to someone else to do?

WINNING – Seeing the checkered flag waiting for you just around the bend.

PEACE OF MIND – Allowing yourself to enjoy every step along the journey's way.

Napoleon Hill in his infinite wisdom defined the word *concentration* in this way:

"Concentration is the act of focusing the mind on a given desire until ways and means for its realization have been worked out and successfully put into operation." He further goes on to explain, "Concentration is the ability to think as you wish to think, the ability to control your thoughts and direct them to a definite end, and the ability to organize your knowledge into a plan of action that is sound and workable."

While the word *concentration* has a variety of meanings, we are focusing on the meaning that is centered on the viewpoint of attention. Attention is the process of focusing on one aspect of your environment, pushing all other things/distractions to the far background.

One good habit to develop is to give the proper allotment of time required to actually concentrate. Think of how many times you mark in your calendar to completely focus on getting a project done. It is remarkable how following these guidelines can allow you to live the life you truly desire by beginning to make focus and concentration a habit. Not only can this habit help you to achieve your dreams but also it will also remove stress and discontentment from your life in the process.

Hill in the *Laws of Success* had five suggestions in his formula for maximum concentration. Here is a summary:

1. Put force and enthusiasm into your expression as you form this (or any) new habit. Feel what you think.

2. Keep your attention firmly concentrated on your new habits/path of getting things done. Forget about the way you "used" to do it.

3. Travel over this new way of doing this process as often as possible. Create opportunities for doing so, without waiting for them to arise through luck or chance.

4. Consistently resist the temptation to travel over the old way of doing things. Every time you resist a temptation that doesn't assist your life, the stronger you become.

5. Be sure this is the right path for you. Compare it to your Definite Chief Aim.

Positive autosuggestion (your internal cheerleader of sorts) works alongside your ability to fully concentrate on what it is you want to bring to fruition. It allows your conscious mind to grab hold of a thought or idea and transform it into action and/or a physical reality.

Our environment plays a strong role in our ability to concentrate. For example, if you work from a home office you need to practice the art of concentration even more intensely than someone who has an office outside the home. Home offices can take multi-tasking to a whole new level. Simple things like shutting a door to keep out the rest of the household for several hours can create a haven for concentration.

One of the greatest gifts that I received from Jennifer White's coaching program on time and life management (mentioned in Chapter 3) was the idea of reserving special days in your week in order to get things done. An example of this would be:

Monday—Support and Administrative Work Day

and/or

Tuesday—Marketing Day

and/or

Wednesday

Creative—Creative Day

And so on…

The key is to create the day that focuses on your specific needs. Everything that has to be taken care of on that day goes into a folder with the appropriate day's name on it. So when you get a bill in the mail, you don't waste your time opening it while there are other things to be done – you take care of it on Admin. Day. Then, no more thinking about it, leaving your mind open to focus on the things you really want and need to focus on. The key is to mark it on your calendar just like you would any other appointment so that it does not slip through the cracks.

In conclusion, just as a camera needs the right light to focus, so do each of us. Think of your focus as your light, making sure these components are in place:

Find – a space where you work your best.

Objective – Define the core objective of your attention.

Concentrate – Give yourself the true amount of time you need to concentrate.

Understand – As you visualize your goal for the finished task.

Structure – Create days that give you less interruption and more ability to get done what you actually want to accomplish.

We are each given a limited number of days on this planet – by concentrating on what we want to do the most, we enable the best of the best to happen. Og Mandino, the author of the best seller, *The Greatest Salesman in the World*, shared these words on the power of concentration … "It is those who concentrate on but one thing at a time who advance in this world. The great man or woman is the one who never steps outside his or her specialty or foolishly dissipates his or her individuality."

I invite you to look through this chapter's collection of Victory Letters to look for those things that inspire your mind to get its fill of possibilities and passions as you focus, focus, focus on the *Master Mind Principle of Concentration*.

Receiving a Smile

If the facts don't fit the theory, change the facts.

~Albert Einstein

Happy Monday,

Have you ever done what so many of us do, avoid change? You treat change like a bad disease only to have it happen anyway and then surprisingly it enriches your life? Change does indeed bring the unknown, especially when we get comfortable with where we are in the world.

Last week I had a big change happen when my son Travis got his driver's license. Now this is something we had been able to avoid for almost a full year because he was late in getting his driving permit (Colorado law says you have to have your permit for one year). He had grown miserable about it and had been counting the days until he could take his driver's test.

As his Mom, I had been dreading this change. The thought of my baby (who will be 17 in March) out there on the highways was not something I wanted to add to my Mama's Worry List. But get his license he did and the joy it brought him was amazing.

When we returned home from the DMV he got in his car (which he had bought with money he earned over the summer) and drove away with a smile from ear to ear. He drove himself to school and came home in the afternoon saying he would pick up his sister from cheer practice. I looked at him as if he was someone else's child. Pick up his sister? The same sister he could previously barely even speak to? Not only did he pick her up but then took her to get something to eat!

Suddenly, putting my worries aside, I saw the possibilities and freedom this change was going to make for our family. Having another driver in the family would in fact help me in many ways, keeping me from driving all over the place. Perhaps my backlog of work could get caught up – a wonderful thought indeed.

What changes have you been avoiding? What are some of the things you have said you wanted to accomplish that require change? Will it mean a change in how you think or a change in how you do things? Sometimes the mental changes can be the hardest to make. What would it take to get you off the dime (or quarter) and put this change into effect?

Sometimes if you open your eyes a little wider you can see a change you may have pushed into the background. Sometimes, as in my case, the change might bring a smile a mile wide to someone you love. And with the month of love just a few short days away – what would you be willing to change for yourself or that special someone you love? In the week ahead I wish you smiles as you see your possibilities.

To Your Successes and Victories…

Floating Your Boat

Every adventure is just around the corner.

~Travis Ruskus

Happy Monday,

Yesterday morning about this time we were waking up in beautiful Buena Vista, Colorado with an adventure right in front of us. Ed, Travis, Bailey and I were heading, for the first time ever, together, to go whitewater rafting. While Ed and Travis had gone once before it was the first time we had ever attempted it together as a family.

The result – awesome!

As we headed towards the river I found myself feeling a bit intimidated in my first attempt at this sport. Something new and unknown was right in front of me. Not the most agile sports woman, getting our instructions on how not to drown gave me pause. Was this the right thing? But I knew there was no turning back as we slipped the big rubber raft into the river. My family, along with a nice couple from New Jersey, and Greg, our tour guide, hopped into the raft and we were on our way heading down the Arkansas River.

Of course, the first thing I was very aware of was that it was going to be a chilly ride as the water was a balmy 48 degrees (and yes, we had opted not to take the wet suits). But the sun was shining and it was a beautiful Colorado day. With my oar tightly grasped while I listened very carefully to every word Greg told us, my fear began to slip away into the river and I found myself really having fun! The beauty of the river had captured my excitement to see what was around the next bend.

Well, the rapids did come our way and while challenging, they were also exhilarating! What I found is that we were warmed up enough by getting a little bit of the river under our belts (and in our shorts!) and our confidence was growing. This sport that I had somehow avoided during the course of my life was really a whole lot of fun!

Now a wonderful memory, our river trip leaves me asking myself and you on this Monday morning, what adventures have you been avoiding in your life? Not necessarily on purpose but one (or two) that has just passed you by? You know what I am saying – an adventure that could possibly range from starting a new business to making a chocolate soufflé – something that has appealed to you but never made it to the center of your radar screen?

It sure does seem that the "stuff" of our life can sometimes get in the way and stop us from taking on adventures and trying new things. With that in mind, I challenge you in the week ahead to take a look at what you have yet to do in your life and then plan to do at least one of them in the not too distant future.

Hoping the call of the river – whatever that happens to be – helps you to float your boat!!

To You Successes and Victories…

New Tricks

You can't teach an old dog, new tricks.

~Unknown

Happy Monday,

This morning as I write to you I am sipping on a cup of green tea as opposed to my regular cup of coffee with cream. You could say that I am out to prove this week's quote to be wrong, as I take on the quest over the next two weeks of a "lung and liver" body cleanse. Quite a challenge for me as I must pay very close attention to every single drop of food and drink that I put in my mouth for the next fourteen days straight!

I have also started walking my dog, Samantha (Sam) at a lake near our house again. This week's quote has been going through my mind as Sam and I cruised around the lake. I have been bringing little treats with me to remind her of her trail etiquette and sticking with me so she can remain leash free.

Sam is eight and while a great dog overall, she loves to say hi to every body, human or otherwise, she meets along the trail – some don't want to say hi and she needs to learn, let's just say, to control her emotions. She is in fact learning new tricks and we are having great fun along the way. Yesterday she was so intent on receiving treats she would not leave my side and had me giggling the whole way around the lake. Sam as well as a beautiful fall morning with the leaves changing in yellows and gold, only added to my giggles.

The goal for us this week is to prove the above quote wrong and start learning new tricks. I was amazed as I cruised the aisles of Whole Foods in Boulder yesterday, preparing for the dairy, wheat and chemical-free diet I am about to embark on.

I am rethinking everything now, including snacks during the day and making sure I in fact get my eight-plus glasses of water per day. Add to all of this the fact that I have three other people I live with who count on my culinary contributions and it equals a lot of concentrated effort.

Effort, though, is worth it when you are working towards something that is important to you. In my case my body is very important to me and I know that I must treat it well as it is the only vessel I have to sail in this lifetime of mine.

In the week ahead, during this season of change – what new tricks would you like to learn? What can you do to stretch yourself in areas that you have wanted to stretch out into for a long time coming? Take some time out and imagine yourself there, just like I am imagining how much better I will feel, not to mention the tricks I will learn with whole organic foods that could change my life forever. I'm allowing not only myself but also my family to feel so much better and to increase our chances for optimum health.

Wishing you a week of enjoying change as it happens "organically" around you and as you push forward to make it happen.

To Your Successes and Victories…

Strong Living

Live Strong.

~Lance Armstrong

Happy Monday,

This Monday morning, as I sit here writing to you, I am looking at the yellow wristband my friend Nancy gave to me yesterday that say the above two words, *Live Strong*.

As I had mentioned in a previous letter a few weeks ago our household has been watching the unfolding of Lance Armstrong's 6th straight year of wearing the yellow jersey down the Champs-Elysees in Paris. Yesterday, he again won the Tour de France. It was an amazing week of bicycle racing and watching the determination in Lance to win again. And, oh yes, inspiring, not necessarily to go out and jump on a bike (though it has sparked that in me in the past!) but to be all I can be in life.

Many of the riders, including Lance, wore the yellow bracelets just like the one I now am wearing. The bracelets are an effort by Lance and his non-profit foundation to raise money for a cure for cancer. At one point, I heard a race announcer say that the bracelets must be good luck charms because many of the riders who wore them did very well indeed.

Live Strong… what a great motto to think about every day. It is especially inspiring to have those two words come from someone like Lance who not only overcame cancer himself but also to this point has become a six-time world champion at something so physically challenging as the Tour de France.

Of course, strength is something that needs to be worked on… it doesn't just happen. Whether you work on your physical or mental strength, you have to have a plan of action to achieve the strength you need to live your life to the fullest. Otherwise, we end up just going from here to there without being all we can be.

The other day as I was in the garden doing some dead-heading (removing the blooms that had come and gone) from my flowers, I thought about how important this action is for the health of the plant and the assurance of more blooms as I did this removal. I also thought about how many things in our life stop us from being all we can be because we don't remove the items that slow down or stop our ability to bloom... to be all we can be.

Where in your life have you allowed yourself to get stuck, to not be as strong as you know you have the ability to be? Where are your weak areas? How can you increase your strength in those areas, especially, if these weaknesses are affecting your whole life, the whole person you are today and can be tomorrow?

In the week ahead, I encourage you to make a plan to build your strength in the area of your life that you have been ignoring the most (physical, mental, career, spiritual). A nice form of encouragement is for you to get your own Live Strong yellow bracelet.

By wearing the bracelet (or something similar as a constant reminder of your capacity to succeed), not only will you be reminded you to live strong but you will also be helping those fighting cancer to live strong as well. Personally, I have had four people in my life die from the disease (along with scares from a number of others). I know cancer has touched us all in so many ways. Each of us can make a difference. (Authors Note: Sadly since the time that I had originally written this letter at least 4 more people I have cared about in my life have died from cancer including, as previously mentioned, my own mom.)

Have a great week ahead and, yes, I will say it one more time... *Live Strong.*

To Your Successes and Victories...

Latitude in Attitude

We either adapt to change or we get left behind.
~Meredith Grey, *Grey's Anatomy*

Happy Monday,

Welcome to October! Changing months, changing seasons and this morning as I write to you I am having changing attitudes about my body. Last week I wrote to you about the two week cleanse I had just begun. It was quite a week of challenging myself to drop some habits, habits that were about just popping anything into my mouth.

Now keep in mind I have never dieted in my life. While there have been stages of cleaning up my diet, nothing to this magnitude has ever come into play in the life of Cheri Ruskus: no coffee, wine, chocolate (a girl's best friend) or simple things like bread, pasta or cheese. Yes, they are all gone and I find myself eating fruits and vegetables each day! Not one or two servings of vegetables mind you, but five! Making sure I get all my water in each day! Yes, this has been an incredible feat for me!

To tell you it has been easy would be a big untruth. In fact, last Tuesday night I was ready to throw in the towel! As I cleansed my body it actually felt worse and I was a bit irritable (my family will tell you a "bit" is an understatement). But the support from those who wanted to see me succeed kept me going. It now makes me proud (as well as relieved) to be at the one-week mark this morning. Don't get me wrong, I do see chocolate in my future but I also know that there are some things I am learning about myself. My sincere hope is that through this process I will wind up on a new dietary a new dietary path.

I suppose that the whole point of change is that it takes us on a new path, somewhere we have never been before. Sometimes change is dropped in our lap when we didn't expect it, making it harder to accept, especially life-altering changes such as an illness or the death of someone or something we love. But accept it we must, as we reach deep inside ourselves, rising to the challenge of creating a new way of carrying on each day.

Crazy thing about rising to the challenges is that it enables us to find out new things about ourselves that may have been buried down deep inside us. We are in fact stronger than we think. Take the will power I had last night at dinner, for instance as the family passed around the biscuits! I love biscuits, eyed them lovingly across the table but did not reach for one and cram it in my mouth (I envisioned doing it though!).

The worst thing we can do in the face of change is to ignore it because as this week's quote alludes, it can indeed leave us behind. It can leave us to find ourselves missing out on opportunities that can make us better, stronger, and happier in the long run.

Wishing you a wonderful week ahead full of pushing yourself when you need to and finding new paths along your way!

To Your Successes and Victories...

The Gift of Breath

Remember to Breathe…

~Good words of advice

Happy Monday,

How many times have we heard this advice over the years of our lives? Seems so simple, breathing is something that we will do about 500,000,000 times in our lifetime but because it's such a subtle activity unless we're exerting ourselves we forget to pay attention to it. We just run around in our day taking in air in many different ways.

Last week was one of those weeks when I was running and running and running. There was lots of stuff happening in our life including the marriage of a family friends' son and hosting a Luau. By Sunday morning, I felt like I had been hit by a Mac Truck and spent the day yesterday just trying to catch my breath.

As I laid around reading and trying to not do much, my brain started thinking about some advice that had been given me during the week (didn't have much time to stop and think about it prior to that – how sad) in regards to how breathing can help us deal with the daily stress of our lives. Since dealing with issues with my back recently, some holistic professionals were helping me to get it resolved. The suggestion had been that I take a look at my breathing and how air enters and exits my body.

One thought that came up for me yesterday was looking at meditation and how it helps us to focus on our breathing. My first look at mediation was in the 60s when the Beatles headed off to study with the Maharishi. At the time, I thought they were just sitting around smoking pot (perhaps they were) and didn't understand what it was all about.

Then I remember hearing an interview with Sting not that many years ago in which he said that he tried to meditate about 3 hours per day. He said that it opened up his creativity and helped him deal with the stress that being on the road can bring.

Personally, I'd be thrilled to get in even 10 minutes a day. So I made the commitment to make it happen each morning, starting this week, before starting my day and doing so to help me start my day. This morning I headed out to my garden and watched some hot air balloons pass overhead while I tried to sit still and get my heart into my head.

It was difficult at first because my brain kept thinking about all there was to get done today… time was ticking away. But by forcing myself to relax (again, how sad) and getting into the moment, I was able to open myself up a bit and release some of the pain in my back. So my commitment is to take that time out each day and hopefully carve out more than just ten minutes. That will take a little bit of work for me.

The cool thing about meditation is that not only can it improve our overall health but also it can reduce stress, improve memory and creativity, help with insomnia and even lower high blood pressure. Exercise for the entire body is important but it is also important to exercise the mind.

So as you move about your week think about these words from William Penn: *True silence is the rest of mind; it is to spirit what sleep is to the body, nourishment and refreshment.* Stop and listen to your breath – pay attention to the quality of air you breathe in and out. There are many sources of information on the Internet, in books, etc. to help you learn more about this function that keeps us keeping on.

Have a great week and happy breathing!

To Your Successes and Victories…

Your Mountain Waits

On every mountain, height is rest.

~Goethe

Happy Monday,

I have to grin while writing this week's letter as I think about a cute little new reindeer that has come into my life and garden. He holds the simple little word – BELIEVE – under his sweet little face. Yesterday morning I went to the grocery store early to try and avoid the crowds that seem to be everywhere and anywhere that money can be spent these days.

Walking into the store I saw this reindeer mixed in among the flowers and holiday decorations. It was as if he called my name, and without even really thinking about it much, this reindeer on a stick was in my shopping cart with his cute little face and the word BELIEVE staring at me.

Well, it was an interesting trip around the grocery store… the stick, on which the reindeer's face and the word BELIEVE were on was so long that, as the cart filled, it stayed prominent in my cart. I found myself saying the word over and over to myself. "Believe." It's amazing when a message like that gets through to you. I had started to feel my holiday spirit waning… with so much to do and so little time. The standard countdown to Christmas was wearing me out. Yes, I began to think… it is time to believe! To remember the joy that is needed to be felt, the love, the reason for the season.

And just the night before at a beautiful dinner I saw the quote of this week's letter. What has touched my mind and heart the most, in thinking this through is the combination of thinking about climbing a mountain (there really is a mountain of work between here and December 25th), finding time to rest and believing all the while. My BELIEVE reindeer now stands in the front garden outside my office window. Just in case I forget over the course of the two weeks ahead, it will be my reminder.

Perspective came into place also this weekend with an email update that was sent my way from cousin Lori about her son Brian (whose touching letter is shared in Victory Letter 104 in chapter 11). Brian was hit by enemy fire in Fallujuh and thankfully only suffered a wound to his leg. It happened while he was trying to get his guys out of harm's way.

A lot of gunfire transpired before all was said and done. It happened last Wednesday during the holy day of the Immaculate Conception and Brian felt confident that Mary had protected him from a much worse fate. Again, my thoughts and prayers go to Brian and his mother, Lori and to all the mothers everywhere whose daily thoughts are filled with the life and death worries of war.

I am sending you this week's wish for victory with you the hope that you are finding ways to enjoy simplicity through the complexity of this season. It can indeed be a challenge. I love the words of Dr. Seuss and hope that they carry you through the weeks ahead. "Today is your day! Your mountain is waiting so… get on your way!"

To Your Successes and Victories…

Victory Forward

Live not in yesterdays,
Look back and you may sorrow.
Live precisely for today,
Look forward to tomorrow.

~James Joseph Huesgen

Happy Monday,

Well, it has happened… another year has come and in a few short days it will be gone. We continue to get older and hopefully wiser as the world around us changes on a continual basis.

So here we have this fresh New Year to look at, explore and make ours… if we so choose. While some people find New Year's resolutions to be overrated I find them to be invigorating and a chance to get a fresh new running start.

As I have mentioned, in years past, I like to get a theme going for the year and make up a notebook with goals, hopes and dreams. You know, things like places to go, things to do, things to stop doing, enhancements for my work and life.

I call this my Victory notebook (I can imagine your surprise in this) and it is inspiring just creating it. To make our own, start by clearing your mind of any self-doubt and think about a theme and a motto for the year. For example, my theme for the year ahead, is "Take Flight," inspired by the recent Wright Brothers 100 year anniversary of flight. My motto has been inspired by a bumper sticker I recently saw that read "Well-behaved women rarely make history".

Visuals are a great way to enhance your notebook and can be achieved by taking old magazines (or new ones) and tearing out pictures and words that inspire you. Remember making collages? Simply start tearing and you can make some fun discoveries. Those magazines that were headed for the recycle bin will take on a whole new life.

Break down your goals by month and spend the time imagining your world in the year ahead.

Now share these ideas with your mate or someone close to you who will not only help inspire you to make them happen but will be your coach to insure you stay on track. Another option is to join a Master Mind Group that meets on a regular basis to assist in keeping you focused and on the path to making your dreams, hopes and wishes a reality.

The last and most important step for your notebook before you stick it up on a shelf and forget about it is to keep it somewhere you see it on a regular basis. Then plan a creative time each month to review your progress and to add new items to your notebook as your life evolves in the coming year.

Remember these components in creating your vision for the year ahead:

V – Visualize the who, the what and the why of your life.

I – Imagine the world… as you want it.

C – Create a notebook that reflects your hopes and dreams.

T – Team spirit… surround yourself with people who believe in you.

O – Onward you go making things happen.

R – Revisit your goals and dreams on a regular basis.

Y – You are the one to make this happen… so go for it.

Wishing you much peace, prosperity, happiness and victory in the year ahead! To Your Successes and Victories…

CHAPTER 9

Victory...
And Cooperation

Filling Your Days
with Organized Effort and Energy

Working together—one for all and all for one,
Doing our due diligence as we answer
our true call,
Keeping perspective clear and true,
Side-by-side while achieving fulfillment

oving from the principle of Concentration we head directly into the Master Mind Principle of Cooperation – because let's face it if we don't have cooperation all around us, our ship could easily be sunk! This form of sustainability comes into our lives in many different shapes and sizes, from automated technology services that can assist us in our tasks each day, to the spectrum of people who become our support system. Included in this group of people are not only our business associates and colleagues but also our family and friends. In fact, our family and friends are the foundational support that really can keep us ticking.

As I write these words I think about how my children are shifting and changing more rapidly than I can mentally handle some days. Travis at 20 and Bailey at 18 are coming into their own. It changes my role as their mom and support system on a daily basis, trying to fulfill their wanting and not wanting me in the same breath. It has required that I find my own support system to help me understand the role that I now play as a mother. Having just recently lost my own beloved mother, I could easily let it consume me, but then I would be losing out on all that I have to fully give in this life, all those things that I still need to wholly give to my children whom I deeply love.

I do find myself saying on a fairly regular basis, during this time of transformation in my family, the words of Reinhold Niebuhr: *God, give us grace to accept with serenity the things that cannot be changed, courage to change the things which should be changed, and the wisdom to distinguish the one from the other.*

Finding the support of those around you who "get you" and who give you clarity and peace of mind – especially when you think you are losing it – is vital. I have been blessed with my sisters who, in my dark hours of life, are there to help me stay afloat. In addition, I have had my two best friends from the time I was six, Nancy and Linda. Through the happiest of times and in the times when our pain has taken our breaths away, they are the ones I know I can count on to see me through.

The special people in each of our worlds are the ones we can call night or day, and they are ready to be there for us and vice versa.

There are all sorts of people that make our world go round – some who enjoy helping us along our way, while some others frankly couldn't care less. Our role in putting our arms fully around this principle is in knowing the difference, surrounding our lives and our businesses with people who want to see us succeed. These are the people who enjoy it when they see a broad smile on our face. This is a big key between success and failure.

Have you ever noticed how just being in the presence of some people energizes you? It's that spectrum of people in our lives who "have our backs." One of the greatest blessings to me in founding the Victory Circles was the bringing together of my "Victory Sisters," as we have come to call each other. These women are not only like-minded women entrepreneurs, but they also share the same amount of passion that I do in creating, operating and bringing success to our businesses. Ultimately, of course, that same passion rolls over into each of our personal lives as well.

This Master Mind of ladies offers the best in themselves and allows me to also give the best of myself. This principle combined with the principle of integrity and living by the golden rule (chapter 11), brings a real richness like no other when bringing people together.

So stop and take an inventory of the people in your life who make up your community. Ask yourself these questions:

Who are the ones you can count on continuously for support?

Who are the ones that you support?

Who are the ones that pull at your heartstrings and get you all warm and fuzzy inside?

Who are the ones that make you step up to a challenge?

How did these people come into your life?

How long have they been there?

Which of these people make you laugh and are fun just to hang around?

Understanding when and how you hang out with people who empower you can bring great result through many forms of cooperation in your life.

One of the greatest examples of cooperation in American history was when 57 men came together to write the Declaration of Independence. These were some pretty headstrong independent thinkers. They had to individually and collectively agree not only on the wording to be used, but also how to implement the words to move the ideals they shared for a new nation forward.

The result of their efforts, made with such strong belief and conviction, resulted in a super power that gave our country its initial and long-standing freedom. It also resulted in a document that held such strong ideas and ideals that it has stood the test of time. In fact, it has been a point of reference and a mainstay for our country for over 232 years now. Democracy in harmony is perhaps one of the truest forms of cooperation.

While writing about this I can't help but have one of our forefather's pop off the page for me and stand out from the rest. This person is a shining example of someone who exuded the cooperation principle – thus accomplishing incredible feats in his lifetime. That would be Benjamin Franklin; a man who not only helped draft and sign the Declaration of Independence but who also did so much more. Indeed, he was quite a well versed man who early on in his 84 years of life came to fully understand all that we have possible within each of us.

Ben Franklin grasped life in many ways, from his inventions to his values and character. He so eloquently wrote on a wide variety of topics and ideals. He highly respected diversity in others, including religious basics and beliefs. In fact, at the age of 20 he created what he called his *Thirteen Virtues*, which he tried to abide by as much as possible all of his life. Franklin said that he tried to focus on at least one per week, "leaving all others to their ordinary chance." He believed they made him a better man and able to accomplish all that he did in his lifetime. I am honored to share his "Thirteen Virtues" here.

The Thirteen Virtues of Benjamin Franklin:

1. TEMPERANCE. Eat not to dullness; drink not to elevation.

2. SILENCE. Speak not but what may benefit others or yourself; avoid trifling conversation.

3. ORDER. Let all your things have their places; let each part of your business have its time.

4. RESOLUTION. Resolve to perform what you ought; perform without fail what you resolve.

5. FRUGALITY. Make no expense but to do good to others or yourself; i.e., waste nothing.

6. INDUSTRY. Lose no time; be always employed in something useful; cut off all unnecessary actions.

7. SINCERITY. Use no hurtful deceit; think innocently and justly, and, if you speak, speak accordingly.

8. JUSTICE. Wrong none by doing injuries, or omitting the benefits that are your duty.

9. MODERATION. Avoid extremes; forbear resenting injuries so much as you think they deserve.

10. CLEANLINESS. Tolerate no uncleanliness in body, cloths, or habitation."

11. TRANQUILITY. Be not disturbed at trifles, or at accidents common or unavoidable.

12. CHASTITY. Rarely use venery but for health or offspring, never to dullness, weakness, or the injury of your own or another's peace or reputation.

13. HUMILITY. Imitate Jesus and Socrates.

Leading his life by these virtues, Benjamin Franklin touched and continues to touch the lives of so many through his strong convictions, his writings and his revolutionary inventions. When he died in 1790 at the age of 84, it has been estimated that approximately 20,000 people attended his funeral. This is really an amazing number of people considering the population census for the city of Philadelphia, where he lived the majority of his life, was 28,522 people that year. Indeed, he was a highly respected and well-loved man.

As you move on to read the Victory Letters from this chapter keep these further words of Ben Franklin in mind, "If you would persuade, you must appeal to interest rather than intellect." Enjoy those you spend your days with as you further each other's path towards happiness and success. Remember that no person is an island as you continuously incorporate the *Master Mind Principle of Cooperation.*

Sharing is Caring

The best Victories are the ones you can share.

~Author unknown

Happy Monday,

Saturday was a perfect spring day that gave way to gardening chores and the expectation of the season of spring unfolding all around us. While Ed was in the back yard working hard on a the expansion of the garden (thank you, thank you), I was wandering from here to there taking care of items like getting the lettuce planted and doing one of my favorite things (yes, tongue is in cheek): pulling up the already prolific dandelions.

As I pulled the dandelions from the front yard, I became aware of a very loud buzz getting louder by the moment. The bees in our flowering trees and bushes were busy at work enjoying the essence of the many newly emerged flowers. It was electrifying as they hummed in harmony while doing what it is they do. I could not help but think about how their buzzing brought to light the total essence of teamwork. You know, that energy that happens when more than one person (animal or thing) is working together towards a common goal; an electricity of efforts seems to happen.

Teamwork is an action that is a great thing to watch, hear and participate in. We can see the process of having something new come to life. Perhaps that is one of the reasons I grew to love watching the TV show, "The Apprentice" and was once a "Survivor" fan. In these shows you watch people connecting (or not) and this teamwork is compelling, making all the difference in the participants winning or losing the game. Most compelling to me is the fact that they are complete strangers taking on the challenge of being part of a team in order to accomplish mutual goals.

For the majority of us, we are a part of a variety of teams throughout the course of our life. From our family, to friends, work, perhaps church, volunteer commitments, and on and on… we find ourselves working with others. Sometimes we buzz along making many strides like our friends the bees, and sometimes we hit a wall and find ourselves not working together in a groove and getting nowhere fast.

My kids worked together as a team yesterday afternoon when Travis took on the task of teaching his sister Bailey to skateboard. I was floored as I watched them go for quite a long time interacting with each other... teaching and learning. It's something they don't do very often these days. Of course it warmed my heart and no broken bones was just one of the results of the afternoon of laughter as brother and sister got to know each other a little better.

Perhaps that is one of the life lessons to be learned with teamwork... that we get to know each other just a little better in the process no matter the outcome. Great friendships can indeed be the victory that is won in the end.

What teams are you a part of? What difference does your contribution make not only to your life but also the lives of those on that team? What happens to your energy levels when you work with the teams in your life? What is the greatest team effort you have ever participated in? What were the results? How did it change you as a person?

I invite you in the week ahead to become a full participant on the teams you have committed to being involved with... or move on if a team is not giving you what you need in your world and you just aren't clicking. Perhaps this would be a good time to remember to thank those people who make up your teams!

Wishing you a week with lots of buzzing energy!

To Your Successes and Victories...

Creating a Dream Team

You can't see the picture when you are inside the frame.

~Les Brown

Happy Monday,

The Ides of March are upon us. While it was a pretty lousy day for Julius Caesar it is a wonderful day for me every year as I celebrate the birth of my first child, my son. Happy Birthday, Travis!

This past Friday night I participated in an evening of discovery with a previous client who has become a friend of mine. On this night, she was looking to improve her business. I was extremely proud of her as she brought together about 10 people to help her try to discover new ways to take her business from just breaking even to profitability. It is not easy to stand in front of people whom you know, some whom you don't, include in the mix your employees, and ask for help, admitting that you do not have all the answers. She did it with style and grace while bringing together employees, friends, colleagues, her vendors and fellow business people.

As we began to explore the possibilities of where her business could go, we had to figure out just where she had been, something we all should do on a regular basis. It is difficult, if not nearly impossible, to always take an objective viewpoint of where we are going as we move forward in our careers or in life. A brainstorming group comprised of people who really care about you as well as people who can be objective is truly a great and productive way to go.

Letting go of our opinions about ourselves can be difficult, to say the least. Opening ourselves up to "possibility thinking" can be a little daunting at first, but once you get into it, the possibilities can be fun and amazing. Are you stuck on something in your life right now? Have you pondered it over and over in your brain with little to no results? How about putting together a brainstorming focus team to help you see a new light?

Another good use for this process is to help someone you know who is stuck (assuming they want to be unstuck). Adjust the details depending on the situation, but the keys to having this kind of brainstorming become a success are as follows:

1. Invite a wide variety of people whom you respect.

2. Have food and drink to keep everyone energized.

3. Introduce all parties and explain the reason they were chosen to participate.

4. Be ready to state where you have been and where you want to go.

5. Help everyone be comfortable enough to speak openly and honestly.

6. Keep an open mind, have fun with the process as you listen, listen, listen.

7. Ask several people to take notes to catch all that will be said.

8. Give yourself plenty of time for the process. (We went on until 2:00 am!)

9. Be ready to take action on all the ideas you receive.

10. Send a thank you note to the participants letting them know how you are moving forward with the ideas given (you never know when you may need them again).

None of us are ever alone, though sometimes it can feel that way. People in your life really do care; they are ready to help when you ask. The amazing thing is that others out there who you may not know that well are ready to help you as well. This concept has also been put in play on a regular basis with our Master Mind groups of the Victory Circles. It works beautifully as we get feedback and ideas generated each month on the steps we are taking to move our businesses forward.

So as you move into your week, look at those people who might be willing to be part of your "dream team.". Be ready to use the ideas of others to spark you on your journey. Let your brainstorming open up the path to your dreams! You never know just what you will find!

To Your Successes and Victories...

Touch of Encouragement

Every time we encourage someone, we give them a transfusion of courage.
~Charles Swindoll

Happy Monday,

With Mother's Day less than 24 hours in my past, I felt blessed this year to have been able to spend part of the day with my mother. Walking together to the store yesterday morning to pick up fixings for breakfast before heading to the airport was a special time indeed.

As we walked together through the neighborhood where I spent my teenage years, I was reminded of how much encouragement my mother had given me along my way to get me through those turbulent times. The years of confusion, uncertainty and unknowing, the self-inflicted time of turmoil that teenage thinking brings made it difficult to know where I was going, but with her help, I knew that I was on my way.

As mothers, coaches, friends, siblings, fathers, co-workers, bosses, anyone in some form of leadership, one of the greatest gifts we can give those we love or care about is encouragement. Helping those around us to move forward in life also helps us move forward. It's a win-win situation: we wind up helping each other to become the happiest and most fulfilled people we can be. Encouragement propels us along our path, especially on the steps that seem especially scary or daunting, the ones that make us fear we will never get our feet planted fully on the ground.

Who are the people who have played a part in encouraging you in your life? Who is it that has given you just the push you needed when you found yourself back-stepping without enough spring in your step to move forward? Who is the one person on a dark day that helped you to see the light, to see what was to come instead of letting you slip into what you were afraid of?

During my journeys in California last week I attended the funeral of my dear friend Nancy's beloved Aunt Katie. At 94 years old she had spent her life giving encouragement to her family and friends. Never having children of her own, she had been there for her nieces and nephews with a "can do" attitude that she carried to her dying breath.

As you move forward in your week remember the lives of those you touch along your way. Sometimes it can be something as simple as a smile, a nod or a special glance that can pull someone out of the doldrums. Look up from your life, your "to do's," and give a little perspective to someone who can't see the forest through the trees. Remind someone who is about to give up on a dream just what he or she is capable of achieving – that someone could even be you.

Wishing you a week full of possibilities and courage to move towards those dreams that were only passing thoughts in days gone by. I also want to wish my husband Ed a very Happy Birthday today with a year ahead that brings him joy.

To Your Successes and Victories…

The Ties that Bind

You only live once but if you do it right, once is enough.

~Joe E. Lewis

Happy Monday,

This Monday morning finds me writing to you from the woods outside of Pittsburgh. The uniqueness of the morning is not only the location from where I write but also the coolness that is in the air on this the 2nd day July. As I bundle up with my coffee and computer I am filled with a great fullness in my heart from the past week of my life.

As with any vacation or trip that we plan, I came on this one with anticipation of what would be during the ten days I would be away from home. We have spent these days executing the laid out wedding plans of Ashley and Eric (Ashley is the daughter of my dear friend Linda). Each step along the way I have been able to feel the great sense of love, friendship and family.

While there was a lot of work to be done in preparing for the events to take place, I could not help but feel that weddings are always a wonderful time to re-evaluate the many relationships that make up each of our individual lives. Not only those relationships in our immediate family but those that bring us great joy and satisfaction. It is a good time to stop and look at where different relationships have taken us in the past and where we are going with them in the future.

To watch a young couple plan their wedding day and the life in front of them is inspiring and invigorating. From the time you see the bride walk down the aisle to the final dance at the reception, it is a time filled with so much love. So many things we plan come to fruition in somewhat different ways than we perhaps initially visualized them. The key is to go with the flow and totally enjoy the ride. Enjoy the good with the bad and each day for what it brings to us in our life.

Looking out at the physical beauty around me this morning, I revel in the great friendships that have been near me over the past 10 days. I feel gratitude for this sense of freedom to love and be loved. In just two days we will be celebrating Independence Day and our freedom as Americans to live daily in that independence. It is a good time to open our minds to what it is that we are grateful for in our life today and what we are looking towards tomorrow.

Wishing you a week ahead that brings you the special jewels of time, love and friendship, the ones that make each of our lives so unique and special. As the fireworks shine on 4th of July night, remember the relationships that make your world shine. Ask yourself, who are the people who make your world just a better place because they exist, and what you can you do to enhance each of those relationships? Let freedom ring!

To Your Successes and Victories…

Celebrating Each Other

A wise man will make more opportunities than he finds.

~Sir Francis Bacon

Happy Monday,

Deciding upon this morning's quote made me chuckle as many opportunities are indeed knocking on my door – a bit loudly I might add. This morning's letter is being written a bit late due to several things, or should I say "opportunities," that needed my attention first thing this morning.

Some Monday mornings start with a bang, and we can decide to jump on the wave and hit the crest of it by coffee time – or not. The nice thing is how the choice is usually always ours. This morning I have not only hit the crest, but I am back on the beach (ok, actually in my garden) again sipping my coffee with a smile at what I have already accomplished today!

This week I would suppose what really stands out for me is the number of opportunities we have in our lives. After all, we indeed do live in "the land of opportunity." Yesterday while attending a special ritual for a client and friend of mine who was celebrating her 50th birthday, it hit me that we don't do enough "ritualistic" activities in our busy lives.

You know, the celebrating of moving from one point of our life to the next. Sure, we do it for the big things like weddings, births, deaths and a few religious ceremonies in between, but I am talking about those things like taking the next step into another segment of our lives: a new age, a new job, a new career, a new path or a new place we call home, or even something as awe-inspiring as the new moon we watched come over our backyard last night while sitting out at the fire pit.

My client's celebration was not a typical party mind you, but something with a little more meaning and depth to it. What hit me yesterday in the birthday ceremony was how the Native American founders of this country put a sacredness and genuine thoughtfulness into all that they did. Ritual became almost a daily habit, as if it was a way to share gratitude and thankfulness out loud every day, not only for what they had but also for the gifts of their forefathers and mothers, the gift of life.

Perhaps one of my favorite parts of the event yesterday was the inviting of our grandmothers' spirits to come be with us during the several hours we spent together. The thought of both my grandmothers sharing that space and time with me opened my heart very wide. It reminded me of their love, strength and deep importance in my life. Without them in my ancestry I would not be here.

I also loved the Native American tradition of using corn meal as a cleansing agent. In this ceremony it was used to dry the birthday girl's feet after they were cleaned and massaged by several of her friends in the group. The corn meal was to purify her feet as she started down the new year of her life. What a fresh and positive perspective to take! In addition, everyone took a turn to put a flower or two in her hair – totally transforming her face with a new glow. It was terrific to watch.

This brings me to the question of asking what are the rituals in your life that allow you to show your gratitude and thankfulness? How do you open yourself to keep a clear perspective on your life and the changes that constantly happening around you?

When is it really clear to you that a change needs to happen because you have opened your mind to the possibilities?

Wouldn't it be great if we celebrated each other and the opportunities available in our lives every single day? As you set out for your week ahead I invite you think about these words from Thomas Edison who said, "If we all did the things we are capable of doing, we would literally astound ourselves." Wishing great possibilities in all you do this week!

To Your Successes and Victories…

Welcoming Change

Do what you have always done and you'll get what you've always gotten....

~Author Unknown

Happy Monday,

Ah… change is in the air and as I mentioned in last week's letter the change of season has left Boulder Valley and the mountains beyond blazing with color. The last couple of days were so absolutely beautiful that you could not help but be grateful to be a part of this planet. Times they are changing. It is hard to believe that very soon the 70-degree days we have been enjoying will be gone and winter will be upon us.

As I drove around town this past week the thought kept going through my head that it would be great if all change could have such a glorious welcoming as the changing of the leaves do each year. Yes, we know that after all this glorious color the leaves will be gone until spring… but the truth is the beauty of the change makes us welcome it. And hey, there is nothing we can do about this change because Mother Nature and the powers beyond seem to have it under control. As I write to you this morning I have a rotten cold… good news is that in a couple of days things will change, and it will be gone!

I cannot remember who officially said the above quotation (anyone who does remember… drop me an email), but it has been rolling through my head the past few days as I thought about change. Change… sometimes it just happens, you know, like the change of seasons… change happens. Other times we have to initiate the change, we have to be the one to make it happen… and that can be scary… heading out into the unknown. In fact, fear of the unknown is probably the number one reason people avoid change.

A dear friend of mine is facing a major life change. After 45 years of living in Boulder County she has made the decision to move to Florida to be close to her son and his family. It has been very difficult for her even to think about this change as she loves Colorado… but now that she has, she knows this change is exactly what she needs at this point in her life and her grandchildren will be so blessed to have her near them.

Think about the major changes that took place in your life… did you initiate them or did they just happen? When was the last time you stepped out of your comfort zone to make a change happen? Or maybe I should ask when was the last time you stepped out of your discomfort zone to make an improvement in your life? It is amazing how we can think about a change for a long period of time and then one morning we wake up and know that now is the time. Here are some questions to ask yourself in the week ahead.

1. What change would you like to see in your life within the next 6 months?

2. Who else besides you will be affected by this change?

3. What will happen if you do not make this change?

4. What will happen if you do make this change?

5. Who or what is stopping you?

6. What is one thing you could do right now today to begin the process for this change to happen?

I hope that you address these questions seriously and with an open mind to change in the week ahead, as well as the ability to be grateful for the gifts you have in your life right now, today.

One morning last week, as I was coming back to the house after walking the kids to the bus, I saw a rainbow. How unusual it is to see a rainbow in the morning: it's simplicity and beauty made me run in to get my camera so I could further capture that moment. You see I knew that moment would change and I would have to capture it not only with my camera, but also with my heart, and then let it go.

That's how change seems to happen. Just like the ash tree in our yard that is right now the most beautiful yellow orange and blankets the backyard with it's extra brilliance… in a few days it will change… and there is nothing I can do about it except remember its beauty. Happy changes to you!

To Your Successes and Victories…

Traveling Lessons

Though we travel the world over to find the beautiful,
we must carry it with us or we find it not.

~Emerson

Happy Monday,

One thing for sure is that no matter where in the world we roam there indeed is no place like the one we call home. The other places we travel to can help us discover new things not only about the destination but also about ourselves.

Our trip to Mexico began a week ago Saturday with a 2 am wakeup call to have us on the 6 am international flight. We did it easily as the excitement for the trip was fueling our bodies for the sleep we were lacking. It is funny how excitement and anticipation will give us that kind of energy.

So here in a nutshell is what was learned on our family's Thanksgiving week journey.

OPEN YOUR MIND TO THE POSSIBILITIES.

No matter what the brochures say, the reality of your destination is always going to be somewhat to a lot different. Each new moment brings about possibilities that you may not have been expecting. These can range from the elements of Mother Nature to the creatures in nature. If you are flexible enough to take on what comes your way, you can enjoy the rain or deal with the unexpected bug bites.

KEEP YOUR HEAD IN A POSITIVE PLACE.

Keeping your head above the sand, literally and figuratively, can keep you from wanting to hurt those you are traveling with. In fact, if you stay positive, your traveling companions no matter who they are, truly become your link to fun. One person's lightness can help another through darker moments.

LOOK FOR BALANCE IN YOUR DAYS.

We were intrigued with the pink flamingoes (live, not yard) that hung out just outside the open door restaurant where we ate our breakfasts and dinners. We loved to watch them as they slept, using just one leg to keep balanced, tucking their heads into the feathers of their bodies. They achieved the perfect balance in this effort. Imagine that same kind of balance when traveling and you have the right mix of fun, inner reflection, one-on-one and group connection time. All is in proportion.

BE IN THE MOMENT.

We experienced gorgeous sunsets; Bailey and I swam with the dolphins; and I had some great card games with Travis during both torrential downpours and sunshine on the beach. There were moments during our trip that will last a lifetime. Enjoying them fully in the moment will allow me now to live without sadness or regret that they are over. They fill my heart with happiness and joy.

DON'T GIVE UP.

Perhaps one of the greatest thrills of our trip happened on our journey home. Our flight left Mexico an hour late, leaving little time for the customs process and meeting up with our connecting flight in Dallas. For anyone who has ever traveled through the Dallas airport, you know that it is not the easiest place to move from one terminal to the other.

With a series of unfortunate events, we kept the pace and were literally running through the airport to try and make our connecting flight to Denver. In our tired and hungry state we just kept thinking if we could only make it we would not have to wait in this airport another three hours!

With actually only seconds to spare, we made it to our gate with no one there except a few flight representatives. They didn't even ask for our tickets just told us to take the first row of empty seats on the plane and to run as they were closing the airplane doors.

Well, made it we did! We got into that first row of seats they had saved for us – which just happened to be first class! All of our worries and troubles in getting there melted away as we were well fed and extremely pampered for the hour and a half flight home. The four of us kept grinning at each other all the way. The perfect end to our vacation happened with no planning at all.

As I wind up this morning's letter, sounds of Christmas carols fill the airwaves, snow is on the ground outside my window and onward we go into the holiday season. I wish you the opportunity to use these traveling lessons in your everyday life not only during this time of year but all the days of your journey.

To Your Successes and Victories…

Making a Difference

Increase Peace.

~Bailey Ruskus

Happy Monday,

This Monday morning is finding my brain moving slowly in getting engaged for the week ahead. After a full weekend of holiday celebrations, shopping, wrapping and finally decorating the house, my heart is full but exhausted. But no rest for the weary at this point of the game with Christmas Eve one week from today!

This week, the words "increase peace" written by my daughter Bailey on a chalk drawing on our back patio this past spring, comes to my mind. It's a simple statement that gives the hope call to action for finding more harmony. It seems appropriate at this time of year, when there is so much hustle and bustle, to keep peace in mind.

I look at the lights of the tree this morning and think of the special moments that have transpired over the past few days. These moments included spending some great one-on-one time with my dear friend Nancy who is in town for just a few days. Perhaps that is the greatest gift the holiday season, the opportunity to see and visit with friends and family you normally don't have "time" to see.

This time of year we send out cards and take the time to make a fuss. Sure, it is a lot of work, but oh so worth the effort. There is no doubt about that. If you want to give yourself a true gift of this season in the week ahead then take the time to have some really meaningful connections. This can include some heartfelt conversations with the people in your world or sharing the things and people in your life in a holiday card.

Increase your peace with co-workers, clients, colleagues as well as family and friends. Indeed it is the season. Then, think of ways to implement that peace and goodwill all through the year by having meaningful and honest conversations. What can transpire is amazing when we open up the communication levels – all year long!

Have a wonderful week ahead in the final countdown to Christmas. May your days be jolly and bright!

To Your Successes and Victories…

CHAPTER 10

Victory... And Profiting from Our Failures

Learning from Disappointments and Turning Points

They say what goes up must come down,
All the while keeping our mind at peace.
To better navigate the storms of life,
As harmony and fulfillment is achieved.
All the while guiding the way towards
keeping hopes and dreams alive.

Would you call the rose with fallen petals a failure? Or use the petals to create a potpourri while remembering the beauty of the rose?

This principle outlines a reality that we each hold in common… failures of one variety or another. They are a part of the lessons of life. Part of the truth of the human condition is that harmony and joy are rarely gained without an obstacle or two along the way.

As kids we probably learned the most through our failures. Learning to ride the bike usually came after numerous falls – teaching us balance. As adults, failures come in all shapes and sizes, from those of a personal variety to those that have occurred in our careers and business life. It is how we deal with them and grow from them that make all the difference. The key is getting back in to finish the game when we find ourselves cleaning up the mess of just one segment of the whole thing we call our lives.

It seems appropriate to share with you at this point a failure of my own that I wrote about in my book, *The Victory Letters – Inspiration for the Human Race*. At the time I wrote the book I had just hit what I had perceived as rock bottom in my business life in having to file for bankruptcy. By opening up my heart and writing about it, I found not only healing for myself but for so many others, as they read my story and realized they were not alone. This is what I said:

Between changes in the business climate, a business move in the wrong direction culminated by the events of 9/11, I was forced to realize what I thought was one of the worst things that could happen to me, that I would have to admit to the ultimate financial failure.

One of my life defining moments was the day I drove to downtown Denver for my bankruptcy hearing. Totally mortified that I could not pick up the pieces that had fallen in my financial world I cried most the way there, as I had done for days and weeks prior. I felt like a complete failure. All the successes I had in my business life for almost 20 years were forgotten. I simply could not forgive myself for allowing this to happen.

While walking to the courthouse I spotted a beautiful little Catholic Church nestled amongst the skyscrapers. Running very early for my hearing I decided to stop and say a prayer, a prayer for my mental strength to get me through the morning's proceedings. There, in front of the church, was a line of people. At first I thought they were waiting to get into the church but then quickly realized that they were waiting in line for the free food that was being given out.

Wow, what a revelation that was. Here I was concerned that I would have to deal with this failure and here were these people who didn't even have the money to buy a meal. Walking into the church and sitting down, I was really struck with the beauty and peace it possessed. As I sat and said my prayers I watched those who had gotten their food outside as they sat in the church pews and ate.

I became so filled with gratitude for the life that I had been given. It became quite clear that my family, my home, my health, my whole life… just as it was, was a great success in so many ways. I knew as I sat there that morning, watching them fill their stomachs that my heart and spirit had just been filled with so much more. That morning I was sure to say an extra prayer for those people that they too would find their way.

The strength I had been looking to gain came to me tenfold. The proceedings went quickly and fairly painlessly. I headed home vowing to make a difference and to share the things I had learned along my journey. In reality, it had just prepared me for the next stage of my race."

The strongest lessons learned are sometimes the most painful. It is when we acknowledge the lesson and grow from it we are allowed to fully get back in the game. Getting back and on track and remembering what brought you to the point of temporary failure is critical. If you walk away from it only looking at it as failure and not learning from what occurred it can and has beaten many a promising entrepreneur. It is so important to remember that the fear from the failure will soon disappear but you must… without a doubt get back on the horse.

Only then will you remember the lesson that needed to be learned, and keep the strength that is gained through the process.

Learning from our failures takes strength and tenacity. A pain in your heart from a failure can lead you to new horizons you never dreamed possible. The key is to live your life with your eyes wide open. Ignoring the failure and trying to pretend it never happened can cause it to happen over and over again. Understanding it and learning from it makes all the difference.

Thomas Edison found that his idea for the electric light bulb was going to be a lot more challenging than he originally thought. In fact, as is well documented, it took him more than 10,000 failures to get it right. He summarizes these many attempts with, "I have not failed. I've just found 10,000 ways that won't work." His perseverance gave us an incredible invention that changed the way we live. He summed it up this way, "The brain can be developed just the same as the muscles can be developed, if one will only take the pains to train the mind to think."

Michael Jordan missed more than 9,000 shots, lost about 300 games, and missed the game winning shot 26 times. Would you call him a failure? Michael said on the subject of failure, "I have failed over and over again in my life, that is why I succeed."

Perseverance and persistence are powerful qualities a successful entrepreneur must own. Napoleon Hill shared this principle in this way: "Every failure is a blessing in disguise, providing it teaches some needed lesson one could not have learned without it. Most so-called failures are only temporary defeats."

In the *Laws of Success* Mr. Hill further explained failures as **turning points**. He in fact believed that every person has at least 7 major **turning points** in their life, major deciding moments when we can move forward from lessons learned or get stuck inside of the failure. It is what each of us does to move forward that make the difference between an actual failure and success.

Mr. Hill went on to say, "Failure is generally accepted as a curse. But few people understand that failure is a curse only when it is accepted as such, and few ever learn the truth that failure is seldom permanent. Go back over your own experiences for a few years and you will see that your failures generally turned out to be blessings in disguise. Failure teaches people lessons that they would never learn without it. Among the great lessons taught by failure is that of humility."

So as you reflect on the so called "failures" of your life to date, look and see what turning points came your way that in fact changed things for the better. From relationships that went sour to investments that did not bring the return expected, I am sure that each of us can recall those initial negative results that *eventually* brought about something positive.

Recently I shared a glass of ice tea with a friend and colleague who I had not seen in a long time. As we caught up with the happenings of our lives, she shared how she had finally made the break with her fiancé nine months prior, and that it had been a long time in coming. Two months later she ran into a new man, someone she had known professionally and had not thought twice about it. When he asked her out on a date, she went, finding that first night out with him that she had found in him, her true soul mate. They are now planning a long and happy life together. This is something that would not have happened if she had not accepted the failure of the previous relationship and moved forward.

Theodore Roosevelt summed it up beautifully with these words:

"Far better it is to dare mighty things, to win glorious triumphs even though checkered by failure, than to rank with those poor spirits who neither enjoy nor suffer much because they live in the gray twilight that knows neither victory nor defeat."

Remember as you peruse this group of Victory Letters to celebrate your failures, big and small, as they are taking you one step closer to where it is that you really need to be!

Observe how you have inserted into your life the ***Master Mind Principle of Profiting from Failures.***

Shining Your Light

Our deepest fear is not that we are inadequate. Our deepest fear is that we are
powerful beyond measure. It is our light, not our darkness, that most frighten us.
~Marianne Williamson, *A Return to Love*

Happy Monday,

February continues to pump on... Valentine's Day is now behind us and I
hope you are continuing to do kind things for your heart. Over the course of my
lifetime I have loved the opportunity to be swept away by the excitement of a
movie, leaving the real world for a couple of hours to become a part of someone
else's world for a while.

Remember when the VCR was invented and Hollywood became fearful that
people would quit going to the theatre to watch movies? The fear was unfounded
because the lure of getting out of the house and lost in that huge movie screen
away from the interruptions of your world is just too great.

Wouldn't it be cool to have the story of your life be told on the movie screen
and you actually enjoyed every moment of watching it as well as living it? What
would be compelling enough to get people to watch? Would it be a classic to be
watched again and again? What single talent do you possess that people would be
interested in? Or what is that light in you that makes you so special? Is that light
shining as brightly as it could be? What is it that makes your heart tick?

Marianne Williamson continues to write in her book *A Return to Love*, "We
ask ourselves, who am I to be brilliant, gorgeous, talented, fabulous? Actually,
who are you not to be? Your playing small doesn't serve the world. There's nothing
enlightened about shrinking so that other people won't feel insecure around you.
We are all meant to shine as children do... and as we let our own light shine, we
unconsciously give other people permission to do the same."

What do you think it is that you do to make a difference in someone else's
world or even your own? Sometimes it is really difficult to step out of our comfort

zone to make the difference, but once you do… wow… it feels great, and not just for you but also for the people whose lives you touch. Just like watching the movie about someone else… you create a compelling story to be told.

The most amazing part of watching someone do something they truly love is that it comes straight from the heart before anywhere else. Let me ask you these questions:

What is it that you really love to do that allows your light to fully shine?

When was the last time you allowed your light to shine?

Who benefits the most from your light shining?

How could you make that light shine for yourself and others every day?

In the week ahead ask yourself these questions and then write down your answers. Don't just read this letter and say to yourself… yeah that sounds great and move on. Take the time to fully discover what it is that will bring your heart and the heart of others into the light.

Wishing you a week of shining moments! Remember… Lights, Camera… Action!

To Your Successes and Victories…

Regaining Spirit

Nourishing a broken spirit can be a lot of work.

~Sponge Bob Square Pants

Happy Monday,

This morning as I look at the world from the perspective of a new week, new beginnings, I can't help but think that defeat is never easy. Last night, watching the Rockies get swept in the World Series was a bit painful but as with winning, losing holds its own chances for future victories. That, I do know in my heart, is what separates the real players from those who just show up at a game; they don't let a loss devastate them. They just keep on going.

Think about how many times you have lost at something, only to have it make you stronger and wiser. The fascinating thing about baseball and professional sports in general is that just because they lost doesn't mean the team is going to quit playing altogether. Heck, no! They will fine tune and refine their game. The Rockies will be back in the spring with a fresh new season in front of them, remembering they were the National League champions – a feat they had never accomplished before. Next year they can take on the world.

Yet how many other things in life get people to quit when they lose just a single stage of the race or game? Perhaps looking at those who start a business is one of the best examples. Just a few days ago I was talking with a colleague on how easily people can give up on a business idea barely giving it a fair chance to survive. They get bitten by the entrepreneurial bug and are so excited about the prospect of the idea. Then, when the going gets tough in the trenches of getting the business off the ground, they walk (or run) away from it. The statistics for failed business start-ups is proof enough of that fact.

So when do you know when to walk away from a losing proposition? When is it time to say enough is enough, to determine whether the path you are on is too painful to continue or even worth it, for that matter? Funny, as we watched the game over the weekend we kept changing the channel when the scores were getting really painful. But we never completely let our hope or spirit die or said we would never watch the Rockies again.

Looking towards the positive, that light at the end of the tunnel, is all any of us can do when things aren't going our way or as planned. Sometimes, we too need to fine tune the way we are playing the game – as I am sure the Rockies will be doing. But like the old saying about not throwing out the baby with the bath water, remember the wins and fine-tune yourself to handle the losses.

My seventeen-year-old son has left many of his childhood things behind but one thing he still loves is Sponge Bob. One morning a few weeks back I heard Travis laughing at the ongoing antics in Bikini Bottom. Stopping what I was doing, I heard the words for this week's quotation as Sponge Bob helped his friend Patrick through a tough time. Indeed, it is a lot of work to pick up your spirit and get back on the road again. Doing it with humor and light can most definitely be a much better way to go. It helps you to find sides of your inner self that you may not have known existed.

So as you move forward in your week ahead remember that the spooky times can allow fear to get in your way. Give all you have to give, do your best and enjoy the ride along the way! Don't forget to stop and give a kind word to others who may be dealing with their own losses.

To Your Successes and Victories…

Internal Hurricane

You find the only things you regret are the things you didn't do.

~Zachary Scott

Happy Monday,

As I write to you this morning I am filled with the awareness of change and acceptance of allowing change to happen. Looking towards my garden, my beloved zinnia bed is empty after I pulled out the fading flowers over the weekend. This is a hard time of year for a gardener in zones of the country that will feel the frosts of winter. Even the cool nights of fall are more than many of the flowers can bear; my beautiful zinnias were no exception.

Yes indeed, change is constant in our world. Last week I wrote to you about my resistance to listening to the news these days. Well, I was shocked over the weekend as I read in a business magazine about the death last Monday of Anita Roddick, the founder and spirit behind The Body Shop. I almost missed the story completely as I was quickly thumbing through the publication, but her picture and the caption "Green made Good" caught my eye. She has always been an inspiration to me – the entrepreneurial woman who lead a company to great success, never letting go of her ideals and beliefs.

The article left me wanting to know more because it was very dry and matter of fact. So I went to The Body Shop's site and subsequently the Anita Roddick site to get the full sense of the woman and the legacy she has left behind. Perhaps the most compelling words I read came from her grown daughter, Sam Roddick, who wrote a beautiful tribute in honor of her mother: "My mother was like a weather system, she reached every horizon and every corner of the world."

Sam went on to say, "Mum was that hurricane, that tornado, she was that light rain that glistened in the sun. She was the calm wind that blew through my hair, she was the sun kissed rays that warmed by back. My mother was a weather system you could never predict – she was the raging waters and she was a person you could never resist."

At the young age of 64, Anita Roddick left this planet entirely too soon because, crazily enough, she contracted hepatitis from a blood transfusion she received while giving birth to Sam over 30 years ago. The legacy and spirit that she brought to this planet will live on for generations. Beyond her ability to take an $8,000 investment and turn it into millions and millions of dollars, her care and love for the planet and the people on it is most legendary. She touched the lives of so many people across this planet, something we each can hope and aspire to achieve.

For each of us, it is important to remember to get out there and give our all as we let our spirits shine through. One of Anita's favorite quotations was from Elmer Dewitt who said, "If you think you are too small to have an impact, try going to bed with a mosquito." She loved that thought so much she has the quotation displayed on The Body Shop's delivery trucks in England.

So as I say goodbye to my zinnias, I can only promise my garden and the gardener in me that next year they will be even more spectacular than they were this year. As we say goodbye to Anita Roddick, a woman I never knew personally but admired from afar, I will carry the essence of her ability to remember her own spirit every day. Everything and every person have a purpose – we just need to remember to carry it with us and bring it out to play, every single day.

In the week ahead I hope that you can appreciate the beauty of the change around you and how what you do can affect the lives of others.

Wishing you the strength to feel your own wisdom and internal power!

To Your Successes and Victories…

Lessons Learned

If you can't stand the heat, get out of the kitchen.

~**Harry Truman**

Happy Monday,

Summer is for sure sizzling along. On Saturday I found myself at an outdoor event and the 95-degree heat of the July day got the best of me. Only the company of the woman I shared my tent with and the people who visited our tent throughout the day kept me from running and screaming for the nearest body of water or air conditioning. It was hot!!

It is amazing how our determination to see something to the end can get us through a blazing day or the darkest side of night. Over the past nine days the Ruskus clan has once again found itself daily watching the Tour de France and the incredible determination those guys in France have right now. It is really something to see.

A young man from Denmark, Michael Rasmussen, who won Sunday's Stage 9, led the peloton by minutes (a huge accomplishment at the end of a stage) and the commentators doubted whether he could keep up the push… but he proved he could by going on to win the stage. He apparently had this win deep in his mind and the right amount of courage to make it happen. Perhaps the best description I heard for the day was that he was "possessed"… as many of these winning riders seem to be.

On the other hand, it was heartbreaking to hear that the young man who had led the race during the first few days, David Zabriskie, had found the need to drop out after a nasty fall that lost him the yellow jersey several days ago. His body was not working right after that fall and with it went his motivation to keep going.

How many times are we working along towards what we think we want, only to find the fire somehow went out along the way? Or perhaps we find that we are stifling from too much fire from the kitchen and not enough cool breezes along the way? Sometimes the changes and adjustments we need to make are crystal clear (like my never doing an outdoor event in July again!), and other times it takes a lot more to help us find the precise fuel to maintain our fire.

The bottom line is that we will never know until we try. Putting ourselves out there into the unknown is one thing but sometimes changing our course of action can bring about a whole different fear factor to contend with. Now it's easy for me to quickly analyze that the results of my day in the heat on Saturday. My sales a.k.a. my race result – were nowhere near the time and pain it took to make it worth doing again. So, I now know to stay clear of that event; it's one race that does not need any more running. Lesson learned!

Yes, the difference a day can make is huge. Yesterday, I hiked with my family and though it was a tough hike, it was beautiful, meaningful and touched my heart, as I enjoyed being with my husband and children, getting some physical exercise and enjoying the beauty of this place I call home. My race for that day was won.

In the week ahead, try to remember why you went into the proverbial kitchen to cook in the first place… what are you are really cooking? Remember to keep your cool!

To Your Successes and Victories…

Counting Rainbows

I do set my rainbows in the clouds and it shall be for a token
of a covenant between me and the earth.

~Genesis 9:13

Happy Monday,

This Monday morning it feels right to continue on with the theme of happy moments... perhaps even to think of them as rainbow moments. Indeed, several weeks back I shared such a moment with my sister, Robi – yes, it literally was a rainbow moment.

Late one afternoon after sharing some fashion moments with my sister we found ourselves enjoying each other's company over a lovely martini she had poured for us. It was at that moment she decided to share with me some good news about a family member that literally brought tears to my eyes. We hugged each other, savoring the moment only to look out her kitchen window to share in the first rainbow I had seen this summer. It was a moment, a happy moment I will not soon forget.

I was pleased to see in my son's recent pictures from his great Colorado outdoor adventures that he had captured a beautiful rainbow he said was, "like no other I had ever seen." The question does become do we appreciate rainbows when they are handed to us? Do we sometimes just miss them completely because we are too busy or just not really looking?

My daughter and I have always had a special place in our hearts for the song *Somewhere Over The Rainbow*. It became "her" lullaby song when she was a little girl and even now when she wants to feel soothed she loves hearing it (not necessarily by me anymore). Recently, she shared with me a beautiful rendition of this classic song by an artist I had never heard of, Israel Kamakawi. It is something you might want to take a listen to when you get a chance.

I love the words, *where troubles melt like lemon drops...* a soothing thought indeed.

Interesting enough that when I went to Itunes to download this song there was not only the song from Mr. Kamakawi, but also over 60 other artists who have recorded it from Patti Labelle to Willie Nelson to Tony Bennet. The essence of this song seems to have touched many. It is pleasing to know that these artists have in turn touched many more.

Here's to all the special rainbows we can see, share and create as we move forward in our week ahead!

To Your Successes and Victories…

Determination Smiles

Let me win but if I cannot win let me be victorious.

~Special Olympics creed

Happy Monday,

Ah, victory… there is that word again, the one that inspires thoughts of winning and images of achievement. Imagine this and I apologize in advance because this is a little gross first thing on a Monday morning but… we each have it… a shower drain that goes unattended and fills with hair (and other unknown yucky substances) that unbeknownst to us begins to create a "clog." Then, one morning, we are taking a shower and the water just will no longer drain the way it once did. You watch in disbelief as the water that once flowed past your toes now starts to creep up on to your foot.

Yes, we have built a wad of crud and gunk that we weren't even aware we were building. Ever had that happen to you? You look, you see the problem and you just want to ignore it, but as the water spreads over your feet, you know… something has to be done. Do you put it off until a major problem arises? After all, what's a little extra water in the tub? Or do you grab the Drano and quickly try and resolve the problem?

This past Saturday I attended a play that my niece Katie performed in. The story of Oz came to life on the stage as Kate, along with the other kids in her middle school, recreated the travels of Dorothy, Toto and the traveling companions they met along the way, the Scarecrow, the Tin Man and the Lion.

Talk about a group of characters letting problems build! But here comes Dorothy, the problem solver who pulls it altogether and helps each one find the piece of themselves that they had lost along the way. They travel to see the great OZ, who only reminds them that the one they really needed to count on all along was themselves, not looking for that magic "fix" that is somewhere over an undisclosed rainbow.

Perhaps this is a reminder to ourselves to live in the moment, not ignore our problems, or let them become so big that they overwhelm us. It is a reminder to take the gifts and talents that we have developed along our way and to use them, be present with them, be grateful for them.

Victory is in our hearts, whenever we let it in. Sometimes the clogs stop us from letting the water flow. My wish for you in the week ahead is to take whatever adversity you may have in your life and see beyond it. Be grateful for today and what is working in your life. That, in fact, is really one of our greatest Victories.

This week's letter began with the quotation from the Special Olympics. Think about it, here is a special group of people that started their race with challenges some of us can only begin to imagine. And yet, they continue on with determination and a smile… makes you start to wonder how bad your clog really is!

Wishing you a week of joy and peace ahead!

To Your Successes and Victories…

Extra Hugs

Distance has no meaning. The heart always finds its way home.

~Flavia

Happy Monday,

Here we are in the final countdown days before our Christmas celebrations. This past Saturday, I forgot about Christmas and everything else in my life as a routine walk with my pooch and my daughter at a local lake trail reminded me of the importance of those we love in our lives.

There we were, just a few minutes into our walk, when Sammy, my dog, had the "need to relieve" on the trail. I scooped it up in the bag I had with me and Bailey said, "Mom we can't carry that around the lake with us. I am going to run it back to the trash can." Ok, I thought, no big deal. Off she went the very short distance and I slowly walked and played with Sam who was busy greeting other dogs walking along the trail.

Ten minutes passed and Bailey had not come back… very strange, I thought, and I walked back to the parking area where the trash was located. No Bailey anywhere in sight. My mother mind took over and I began to rationalize where she could possibly be and I looked and looked while calling her name. No Bailey anywhere. Twenty more minutes passed as I began to think of the craziness in our world and that someone had taken my baby (ok, so she is 11 but will always be my baby girl). I looked at the frozen lake for any breaks… just where was my daughter?

The tears started coming as the sun was going down and it would be dark within twenty minutes and I had no idea where she had gone. I decided to circle the lake and see what I could find. Then there was a sight I shall never forget… the sun rays shooting up over the mountains as it was sinking and, there across one arm of the lake waving her arms, jumping up a down with her pony tail bopping, was my Bailey. We ran towards each other and holding her never felt quite so good.

Turns out that for whatever reason she did not see me when she ran back from the trash can and decided to go around the lake in the opposite direction and meet me along the way. We both were scared and hugged each other tightly as we finally finished our walk around the lake... much to Sammy's delight.

My wish for you in the week ahead is to look closely at those you love and be grateful for having them in your life. Give extra hugs and let them know how deeply you appreciate the gift they give you with their love. While giving presents is a tradition we have built around Christmas, knowing you are loved and giving love is indeed the most priceless gift of all.

May your holiday be magical, and remember to let the child in you shine!

To Your Success and Victories...

Year's End

The future belongs to those who believe in the beauty of their dreams.
~Eleanor Roosevelt

Happy Monday,

Is it possible in only a few short days December 1st will be here? Of course, the answer is yes… leaving us only 31 days until the year ahead arrives. Remember last January and the dreams you had for this year, the hopes of what this year would bring to your life and your world? I had an interesting question asked by the editor of the newspaper I write for as she was asking everyone at the paper to answer the question, "What have I learned this year?"

I laughed this week after contemplating this question and then hearing during a teleconference another quote of Eleanor Roosevelt's: *"You want to learn from the mistakes of others because you won't have time to make them all yourself."* Interesting… learning lessons, believing in dreams….

Watching my children grow, the reality comes each day that there are some lessons they must teach themselves. No matter how many times I remind them to wear a coat on a cold day it will be the day that they are just so cold that the lesson will be learned. My prayer is that their lessons won't be too painful and that I will be a source of comfort for them.

So the good news is that at the beginning of every December we have 31 days to potentially change the outcome of the year ahead, whether it be the bottom line of our business, taking a look at our tax situation and where we need to be to keep more money in our pocket, or taking a look at where we want to be with our lives at the end of the year.

Ask yourself these questions pertaining to the past 11 months…

1. What are the successes I have achieved?

2. What are the lessons I have learned?

3.   Whose lives have I touched?

4.   Who has touched my life?

5.   What detours did I have to take along the way?

6.   What is important to me to complete by the end of the year?

7.   What obstacles do I need to remove?

8.   Who can help me along my way?

9.   What is mandatory that I complete by the end of the year?

10. What are my dreams for the year ahead?

December is the season of believing… whatever that means to you. I invite you to put on your believing hat and make that which has not happened… a reality.

To Your Successes and Victories…

CHAPTER 11

Victory...
And the Golden Rule
of Human Conduct

Giving Ahead of Receiving

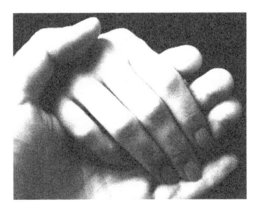

Opening my mind to the awareness,
What I think, feel and see,
Everything as it is in my life,
At this very moment,
I know is a blessing to me.

As we roll into the final chapter of this book the time has come to reflect on the final Master Mind principle in our exploration within the confines of this book. Sure, it may seem simple when you think of the basic essentials of living by the Golden Rule. You do good and you do the "right" thing for all the "correct" reasons, then it all comes back to you with good karma and light—period end of story. Right? Or is it?

Perhaps the hardest part about being of the feminine gender is that sometimes kindness can outweigh logic. Thus, the reason I think that women tend to make less money than men. The "softness" and overactive acts of kindness of the feminine gender can directly influence not only the pocket book but also the ability to run a fully profitable company.

For those of us in the business world, we know that things do indeed change, and they can change seemingly overnight when we deal solely with commerce and profitability. I suppose that this requires the need to have a commercial consciousness at a level just a bit higher than human consciousness. Yes, a little something extra that assures not only that you sleep at night, but also that your sleep is covered with the security blanket made from making ends meet and finding great success.

Ok, so we know the task at hand in business is to be wildly successful and profitable. How do we move forward when some days are much more challenging than others? How do we give when sometimes we feel so much gets taken from us on a daily basis sometimes?

According to the Master Mind principles that Napoleon Hill first discussed, moving forward requires looking all around us in order to get the full picture, to assess that the pieces of the puzzle are being put together basically in proper order. For example, we all want to get good deals in the marketplace, but what if your "good deal" actually meant a hardship to another who had to produce it for practically nothing? Or worse that it was made or sold at a loss? Who wins then?

On the other side of the coin we want our services to be perceived as a good value to others and to be affordable at the same time, creating that win/win as we increase our own bottom line while increasing the bottom line of another.

As with so many things in life, it comes down to balance. John F. Kennedy said, "In giving rights to others which belong to them, we give rights to ourselves and to our country."

Interestingly, while putting together the words for this book, the book, *The Guide to Happiness*, found its way to my desk. Written in 1960, author, Dr. Maxwell S. Cagan had much to say about people being miserable and unhappy. Unhappiness indeed can lead one to no longer living by the Golden Rule. Dr. Cagan had a 15-step process for getting out of the rut leading to "solitude and loneliness." Here is my interpretation of his 15 steps:

1. Have no expectations for always getting red carpet treatment or special consideration every time you go somewhere.

2. Don't show your disapproval or put "your nose up in the air" for things that don't really concern you.

3. Eliminate the habit of always singing the blues and burdening others with your troubles. Sure once in a while is ok, but note if it is starting to happen on a regular basis.

4. Do not judge, jump to conclusions, or make assumptions about other people without first considering their prospective.

5. Trust people without thinking they are out to get you.

6. Have a good attitude while not being overbearing. Learn how to win friends and influence people.

7. Remove negative conversation from your vocabulary including snide remarks and sarcasm that puts down others.

8. Give freely. Stop expecting something in return every time you give.

9. Take an interest in others around you and what they are doing.

10. Be careful not to give away too much of yourself – leaving your reserves empty and unable to fulfill promises made.

11. Look for ways to repay those who have given to you out of the kindness of their heart, even if it is a simple thank you.

12. Think through things you say that might be hurtful to others. Find a way to say things that will have an impact, yet is not insulting or insensitive.

13. Get excited and let your enthusiasm build even when you are engaging in something you might not care too much about, for the sake of someone else or others in the group. Especially, if the activity is important to them.

14. Learn the art of forgiveness. As you learn to forgive, repair broken bonds in mandatory relationships such as those co-workers or family members (people you have to get along with), you will find it will bring you peace of mind.

15. Aspire to come to wholeness with our own spirituality. Take the journey inwards to fully understand your purpose and place on this planet.

The Golden Rule can be yours to have and to hold if you live with an attitude of gratitude. At the beginning of this book I shared how the Victory Letters were created as a reminder for myself each Monday morning to be grateful for all the moments of my life. What I have found after nearly 10 years of writing them is that many of the realities of my life are true in others lives as well. The details of each of our lives are diverse but our loves, passions, hopes and dreams are the connecting fibers for us as humans traveling together on this planet.

Celebrating those things that bring us joy is one of the simple pleasures of life. It's the "stopping to smell the roses" aspect that makes our life joyous no matter how big or small our bank account might be on any given day. No matter how dark the day, our light really does come from inside of us. It has been said that starting every morning with an attitude of gratitude can easily change the perspective on how you look at each day.

When the happenstances of your daily life are joyful, then they can easily be reflected in simple acts of appreciation. Little things, like giving a smile to someone, as trite as it may sound, can become an act of gratitude. Your small action of smiling not only will brighten someone else's day, but your day as well.

How many people, whether you know them or not, do you smile at on any given moment of any given day? It is amazing to watch even the grumpiest looking person's whole face light up and become softer when they smile.

When you start to feel that you are drowning in the things you don't want in your life, try to stop and remember the things that are good and right about your life. Even in the circumstance as painful as losing someone you love to the ultimate goodbye of death – simply honoring and remembering the wonderful aspects of what they brought to your life is something that can bring gratitude.

Gratitude is something that comes from deep within. However, if you find yourself lacking the emotion of feeling grateful – take it one step at a time. Find little things you can do to acknowledge what is right in your life. Keep in mind that I started writing the Victory Letters when things were not going so well in my life – when I was having a hard time feeling very grateful – yet I knew there were many treasures in my life that I was missing out on. The goal for me each Monday morning was (and still is nearly 10 years later) to sit down and find something in my live worth not only writing about but also to feel a sense of gratitude about. Not too surprisingly, I always have been able to find something to write about when I put my mind to it (and sometimes even when I don't).

Even in the dark days of watching my mother struggle through cancer I found that appreciating what I had been given in having her for 52 years of my life brought words to paper that I will cherish all the days of my life. There was only one Monday that was days before she died – when it had fully hit me that she indeed not going to be with us much longer that I simply could not find the energy to write. Instead I cried and cried and cried some more. But in homage to my mom the following Monday morning, two days after her passing, I wrote this letter, entitling it – Peace and Light:

Happy Monday,

"A mother's love is the fuel
that enables normal human beings to do the impossible."
~Marion C. Garretty

As I begin to write the words for this week's Victory Letter I am sitting in my mother's backyard, next to the pool that she loved so dearly. Sipping my coffee, the buzzing of a hummingbird reminds me that life goes on—though mine has changed so completely. On Saturday evening a little before 6:50 pm, just hours before the summer solstice, my beautiful and wonderful mother took her final breath in this life. After nearly three years, her battle with cancer is now over.

The course of the last several weeks, helping my mother go from the hospital to dying at home in her own cozy bed, will be with me all the days of my life. With my siblings by my side we knew the end was eminent and the goal was to make our mother as comfortable as possible. Conversations were had with her that will now have to last the rest of our lifetimes. It was amazing as friends and family from all over came to visit her. It pushed her from only having the couple of days the doctors had predicted to lasting a couple of more weeks.

My mother created a rather large family with 10 children total. Four of us that she gave birth to and 6 that she took in as her own when she married my step-dad. The logistics of all of us coming together again over these final days of my mother's life was a bit daunting to say the least. Friends of my mother loaned us motor homes that we have been camping out in over the course of the past nearly three weeks. Dinners would be in numbers as high as 20 people and simple necessities such as getting an open bathroom were a real treat.

It was interesting the dynamics that came into play—with all of our emotions pretty raw, feelings got hurt and arguments ensued. My mother, in her constant motherly way until the end, lined up a number of her grown children one day at the bottom of her bed, myself included. She wanted to make sure by having us at the bottom of the bed that she could see each one of us clearly. She reminded us that communication was so important during a time that she knew was incredibly hard on all of us. There she was unable to even get out of bed—reminding us that she still knew how to use the paddle. Each of us knew she meant it.

Her strength even in the last hours of her life reminded me that I am who I am today because of her. The pain in my heart is deep, yet I know that I must carry on because that is the way she would want it. And not just carry on at a simple pace but giving my life all that I was meant to give. Somehow with her gone, through the clouds of my tears I can see that she will continue to be my strength moving forward.

Watching her take her final breath, in peace, surrounded by those who loved her was perhaps the darkest hour of my life but through it, in the grace in which she left this planet, the light of her life shined through.

My Mom used to always say whenever we would leave from a visit here, "Don't be sad that it is over, be happy that it happened." Wise words indeed—from a woman who I had the honor of knowing so well.

While she was in the hospital on and off over the past few months there was something that she did that will forever fill my heart. Whenever there was a new baby born in the hospital, some notes from Brahms lullaby would be played over the speakers that went throughout the hospital. No matter what my mother was doing—what discomfort she was in—she would get the biggest grin on her face. She would give a high five to whoever was in the room with her and make a sign of the cross—blessing the new life that had just come to this earth. That really was just who she was and how much she loved life.

In the week ahead I wish you peace and light—appreciating with grace, those that give you strength in your world. Those that are here today as well as those whose light still shines within you, though they may not physically be with you each and every day. Let their legacy become a part of who and what your life is all about. We are all a part of each other—a part becoming the whole.

To Your Successes and Victories!

I encourage you to try writing your own form of a Victory Letter as you travel along your journey. This positive form of attitude adjustment and honesty with yourself can bring balance and lead you gently through the ups and downs of life.

Where to begin?… First, think through what is currently happening to you or through you in your life right now and ask yourself these questions:

What is working and humming along in my life right now?

Who are the people that contribute to the hum?

Of those people, who supports the very essence of who I am and who I want to be?

How do I best honor and support the people who honor and support me?

How do my day-to-day activities contribute to my victories along the way?

What lessons have been laid out before me that I can see and feel?

There is a power in feeling gratitude, but another power is achieved when we actually write about it, when we openly express our feelings either on paper or the computer screen. We each know how good it feels to receive a heartfelt written thank you from someone, especially when we have given a gift that felt important for us to give. It adds another dimension to the thought of "give and you shall receive." Think of showing gratitude in writing to yourself or to others as your way of saying a heartfelt thank you.

Mother Teresa was well known throughout the world for her power of giving. Her words sum it up simply: *"Let no one ever come to you without leaving better and happier."*

As you read the final Victory Letters of this book, remember to connect the essential moments you have been given. From the little moments to the big moments, each and every one matters because they are *your* moments. To graciously hold the moments you have been given in your head and in your heart allows you to savor the smallest of victories. The gift of life itself is a Victory – enjoy each and every moment that you can, as you fully embrace the **Master Mind Principle of Living by the Golden Rule**.

Smelling the Fragrances

Our normal human tendency is to enjoy life,
to play, to explore, to be happy, and to love.

~Don Miguel Ruiz

Happy Monday,

This morning's Victory Letter finds me writing from my garden enjoying the beautiful fragrances in the air! From jasmine to lavender, they are filling my senses. Yesterday, as I floated in our pool, I found myself re-reading Don Miguel Ruiz's book, *The Four Agreements*. It was a wonderful reminder of four fundamental truths in each of our lives.

In sharp contrast, last night I found myself watching a program on the endangered orangutans of Borneo. It broke my heart to see those sweet little creatures whose eyes seemed to gaze so deeply and with such knowing at those who were ensuring their safety. With poachers and people destroying their habitat, their world has been quite shaken, leaving these creatures that had once thrived in their environment to struggle from the brink of extinction. It was especially painful to watch the babies who had lost their innocence along with their mothers when they were only a few weeks old.

As Mr. Ruiz reminded me, we each start on this planet with a clean slate. As young children we are free and excited about the happenings of the world around us. It is what happens in each of our lives as we grow, that form who and what we become, sometimes for the good and sometimes leaving us tainted and scarred by our environment.

We have the choice to let our not so perfect world bring us down or to rise above it and continue to enjoy who and what we have in our lives. Unlike those unfortunate baby orangutans, we have many more choices, even to live our life with values as simplistic as outlined in the Four Agreements, which are:

1. Remember to always have the highest integrity. Believe in the power of keeping your word.

2. Change the internal conditioning of stopping yourself by taking life's happenings too personally.

3. Never assume! Get the facts and make wise choices based on what is real, not on what has been perceived without enough information or even correct information.

4. Give 100% of your best self-possible each and every day.

We have been watching a little family of robins in our yard as the mom has been teaching the little ones how to eat, fly and become independent creatures. Ed and I have been a bit concerned about how these little now "teen-age" robins are going to make it with so many dangers around them. But we know that nature and their doting mother will help them to find their way.

I hope as your week unfolds that you allow for the simplicities of life to shine through when complexities arise. Stop and allow the individual fragrances of your life to fill your senses. Remember to truly enjoy your life in the ways that suit you and the world around you best!

To Your Successes and Victories…

Bright Side of Life

Build a bridge and get over it.

~Amanda Gore

Happy Monday,

This morning for some crazy reason I woke up thinking about right and left-brained people and how our differences make us so interesting... yet challenging at times.

Having spent the last four days at a motivating, informative, fun and heart-warming conference in Kansas City, my head this Monday morning is spinning with ideas and wondering which foot to put forward in the week ahead. The thing I know for sure is to take what I have learned and put it into action before it fades into the dark caves of my mind!

On Saturday morning we were entertained and enlightened (actually lightened) by Amanda Gore, the woman responsible for this letter's quote. She was funny and informative. After one and a half hours she had us feeling pumped and ready to be happy. She ended her session with a sing-a-long to the Monty Python song, *Always Look on the Bright Side of Life* written by Eric Idle. I encourage you to take a look online and sing along to this song that starts with:

> *Some things in life are bad,*
> *They can really make you mad,*
> *Other things just make you swear and curse,*
> *When you're chewing on life's gristle,*
> *Don't grumble,*
> *Give a whistle*
> *And this'll help things turn out for the best.*
> *And... Always look on the bright side of life...*

Go ahead and sing this song out loud and imagine 2,000 people signing it together as we swayed from side to side. It is guaranteed to help you take a lighter look at the world around you.

I hope in the week ahead you can find the brightness in your life and let the other things go. You will feel lighter for sure. Wouldn't it be great while you were at it to make others feel lighter too? Give it a shot and remember that those who take on a lighter attitude towards life have been known to live longer happier lives... Isn't it worth a try?

To Your Successes and Victories...

Heart and Soul

Remember to stand tall and meet the world with your heart.

~Dr. Sid Wolf

Happy Monday,

The beauty of fall has once again transformed the trees to shades of lime green, orange, yellow and red. If you are an autumn color person, this is your time to shine! Don't waste a moment indoors… get out and enjoy the beauty that is in the trees all around us… the colors will be gone before we know it.

The words of this week's quote were said to me last week after a treatment I received for getting my back issues under control. The treatment itself was incredible, making my back feel better than it has in quite a while, and these words reminded me to do just what the doctor ordered… let my heart lead the way.

Think about it… those days when your world starts to get to you crazed or down… where are your shoulders? Hunched, perhaps? Could you be pushing your feelings back and continuously allowing for your heart to not lead the way, as it should? Look at yourself right now as you read this letter. The week has just begun… where is your heart? What if you used this creed in the week ahead and put your shoulders back and met the world with your heart… standing tall? No matter your actual height… each of us can always find a taller way.

Stand up right now… put your heart forward, your shoulders back, and go out there into your world and let your heart shine! The inches you will find will be all your own! Imagine the gift you will give to others by having your heart lead you.

Enjoy a colorful week!

To Your Successes and Victories…

Calm Seas

Whisper words of wisdom, Let it be....

~John Lennon/Paul McCartney

Happy Monday,

After returning from an early-morning emergency trip to the vet's office, last week I was reminded of the clarity and reasoning of the Beatles' classic song, *Let it Be*, coming from my car radio. Driving back down the road to my home that day, I was hit by the beauty and profound simplicity in the timeless words of this song. Knowing that my pooch was going to be okay (for now) perhaps opened up my heart to hear the words of Lennon and McCartney as well.

The title of the song, just three little words that uniquely tell us to take it easy (another song title, *Take it Easy*, by the Eagles also comes to mind!) is a simplistic reminder to slow down, to breathe, to be – just as true today as it was 35 years ago when it was written.

As I listened it made me think how Lennon and McCartney had such a heartbeat for all of life. As they sang, "When I find myself in times of trouble Mother Mary comes to me, speaking words of wisdom, let it be." The image of Mother Mary came to my mind and instantly calmed me.

Now, some of you who know me well know that I am a recovering Catholic – and I don't mean to offend anyone by saying that (always trying to avoid the political and religious topics!) but it is true. One of the foundations in my life from my days of Catholic school and a Catholic life is the image of the Blessed Mother Mary (perhaps because I spent eight years at Our Lady of Lourdes).

Her image brings to mind a beautiful moment of my life when, a few years back, my daughter, Bailey, received her First Holy Communion. My heart filled over as she stood alone at the alter repeating a Psalm in front of the Mother Mary statue. Standing there in her beautiful First Communion dress and veil, I felt very,

very blessed. I have a picture of Mother Mary right near my phone in my office that reminds me to remain calm during whatever storm may come my way, no matter what deadline I face or what piece is not falling into place in the puzzle of life on a particular day. I also find myself during times of stress or angst saying "Mary, Mary" and it seems to instantly calm me.

It is important, perhaps even critical, that we each have those people in our lives that let us be. They let us be who we are and what we are. They let us blossom and become the person we are meant to be. If you think about Mother Mary, that is exactly what she did; it was her purpose on this earth. Truth be told though, that "someone" does not have to be someone older or wiser – they can in fact be someone younger and lighter – lighter yet stronger in spirit, I suppose.

Personally, while my mother is my calm in the storm sharing her wisdom and thoughts, so is my nephew and godson, Jack. On Saturday, his half birthday (which I cannot help but celebrate because after all it is on St. Patty's Day), he and I spent the day together. Being with him allowed me to release my work life and even forget he fact that I was not feeling so well. He was my calm in the storm, my way of letting it be. At 7-1/2 he sees the world through glasses that help remind me of the simpler things in life.

So this leads me to ask you the question, who are the "Let it be" people in your life? Who are the people that are the calm in the storm that may arise in your day, the people who, just hearing the sound of their voice, do in fact "let it be" making your times of trouble begin to melt away? Who are the people to whom you provide a calm in the storm? Be sure to surround yourself with a picture or some kind of a reminder of these people on your desk at your workplace, or somewhere at home, and don't let a day go by not thinking of them. Give gratitude that they are in your life.

Wishing you a week full of calm seas as spring continues to unfold all around us!

To Your Successes and Victories…

Daily Prayers

I realized you can't help but be touched by what goes on in front of you.
~Annie Leibovitz

Happy Monday,

Well, Thanksgiving has come and gone… bringing us straight into the holiday season. I hope the spirit of the season is building within you. This morning I will keep my words brief while sharing with you, as I promised last week, the words from a cousin who is fighting in Iraq. His words were so touching that I thought it important to share his entire letter. No matter the feelings we may have about the craziness of the war we find our country in we cannot forget those young men and women who continue to fight for the democracy and freedom of others.

5 November 2005

To All:

I write, as promised, a modified version of the first letter I penned but never sent. Letters will probably not follow each other so quickly but things here have finally slowed down. Between acquainting ourselves to this area of operation, the October 15th referendum, and the heightened insurgent activity during Ramadan, October was a very difficult month.

Living conditions here are good. We live at an abandoned Baathist lakeside resort and the Marines have about 5 men to a cottage. Chow is good and mail comes regularly. Packages tend to get here in 5-10 days, while oddly, letters take about two weeks or more. "Moto-Mail"- e-mails sent and then printed out—come within 24 hours and are a real blessing, keeping everyone in tune with events at home.

The weather here has changed from very hot to quite cool. When we first arrived, temperatures were routinely over 100 degrees. Much has been said of the heat over here, but suffice it to say that once inside an armored HMMWV, sitting in full body armor, windows closed and the heat of the transmission beside your leg, you feel a bit like a chicken in a rotisserie. Goggles fog up, your weapon becomes hot to the touch and you long for even the slightest breeze. The first month in country, the sweetest part of every day was when I re-entered friendly lines late at night, opened my window and felt relief from air that was merely in the upper 90s. Temperatures now are in the low 50s at night and the mid 70s at noon. This would be welcome weather but with it has come sandstorms, occasional rain and a bitter wind that makes everything feel much colder.

The terrain varies greatly, from sparse desert sands to thick palm groves along ancient canals. War has made its mark here. It is like visiting a Civil War battlefield a year rather than a century after the final shot was fired. One is constantly reminded of the timelessness of this place. One morning while watching a road from atop a hill of deep silt, I chanced upon the site of an abandoned archaeological dig. Foundations of small houses, the remains of a well, the worn stone of a pathway, all that remained of those who were here two hundred or two thousand years ago. Other times, we find dilapidated British Enfield rifles and German Hauser rifles, manufactured in Iran, some carrying ammunition bearing a stamp of 1938 with Nazi eagle and swastika on the brass, reminders that we are not the first between the Tigris and Euphrates.

This fight is a difficult one. The challenge is that the war is truly about winning the hearts and minds of the Iraqi people. Fallujah is strategic both geographically and politically. Located east of the intersection of the main road to Syria and the main road to Jordan, Fallujah is the last stop before Baghdad. For the foreign fighter, this is a path of choice. Here, despite fatuous claims of a great bloodletting of American warriors, the Muj lost the battle last year with the spectacularly poor results of every conventional stand against our forces. For these reasons, there is a concerted effort to retain or regain, respectively, control of this area and its population.

Some days our lives are like that of a police officer, others that of an aid worker, others as killers seeking a single target. This constant change of context is not easy. Mistakes and happenstance cause damage quickly; the second and third order effects of each error engendering a negative perception. War is not scrupulous in who suffers. I met a boy who was shot through the knee while asleep on a summer night last year, innocent victim to a gun battle two miles distant between a convoy and the Muj. Another time, we watched an Iraqi vehicle inexplicably careen out of control at high speed, flipping several times. Rushing to the scene, we pulled the man from his vehicle, provided first aid and summoned the police. As we helped this man, accusing eyes peered from every car that passed, blaming us, guilty by association with this accident.

The simplest human emotional response to such events is expression of pity, sorrow and ultimately, resignation to frustrated surrender. It is just such a reaction that the insurgents anticipate and exploit. My Marines have to remain constant professionals, controlling their emotions, managing fear, anger, pity, and boredom; often choosing to kill or not to kill at 60 MPH at night from the turret of a HMMWV. This is an incredibly cerebral battle. It is not easy, especially with little sleep and the exhausting day-in, day-out slog of work, to reason through it all. Absolutes do not work. You can neither sympathetically drop all guards nor angrily point guns in every face.

Every Marine must be ready to be a "Good Cop" or "Bad Cop" at the drop of a hat. Against this, conventional warfare, for all its complexity of maneuver and firepower, seems so much simpler. In a conventional war you can give truth to Tacitus's maxim that Roman conquerors would "make a desert and call it a peace." The existence of a front and a rear, clear enemies, straightforward goals and simple rules make a conventional war checkers to this game of chess we play. I am sure I have said nothing new here, but I believe these challenges bear repeating because despite all we face, my Marines have performed marvelously. Two noteworthy examples I want to share:

Corporal Derek Burchfield from Tennessee was in the truck with Sergeant Adams when he was killed on 15 October. A week later, Corporal Burchfield was attacked again, this time when his vehicle ran over a mine. The armored HMMWV saved his life, but he was wounded in the right leg. Knowing he was hit, he nonetheless continued to lead his Marines, refusing medical attention, hobbling around the wreckage setting security. He did not accept medical attention until I arrived and took command of the scene. Two days later, he begged me to be included in an operation to catch an IED triggerman and off he limped after the enemy.

One of the biggest challenges we have here is the wear and tear on the HMMWVs exacerbated by constant use and the added weight of armor. Without the vehicles my platoon cannot accomplish its mission. Over the last month, three of my Marines, Sergeant Matthew Fontenot from Louisiana, Corporal Markoe Beachley from Maryland and Corporal Justin Wess from Ohio have worked in their off hours, often through the night between back to back patrols, to keep the trucks running. They have learned on the job to rebuild transmissions, replace half shafts, suspensions, alternators and through a myriad of repairs build a "Monster Garage" of vehicles that often resemble a scene from "Mad Max." Without their work, the platoon would have failed in its mission long before now.

I share these stories for two reasons: First, to show the inspiration that these men give me daily. Heroes like these keep me in the fight. They humble me to do my job with the same passion that they do theirs. Second, because the underlying theme I see in my Marines is that of tenacity. It is this same trait that we seek to articulate to both civilian and insurgent through our words and actions. The message is simple: attack us, wound us, kill us, blow up our trucks, we will keep coming back and will only leave when we choose to.

The day Sergeant Adams was killed the platoon was spread over some miles distance. Hearing of his death, I ordered a link-up and we immediately drove back into the area of the ambush. In the final minutes of his life, as he was evacuated, Iraqis along the little dirt road through the palm grove had laughingly mocked the speeding convoy. That afternoon, the second time we left, no laughing was heard behind us but many tears, and three of those involved in his death rode as prisoners in the back of our trucks.

In light of what I continue to see here, I cannot help but find relevance in Winston Churchill's comments about the battle of Gallipoli many years after World War I had ended and the battle, his inspired brainchild, was deemed an utter failure: "Searching my heart, I cannot regret the effort. It was good to go as far as we did. Not to persevere-that was the crime."

All right, enough from me. God Bless, and thanks for keeping me in your thoughts and prayers. For all those who have written me: I will try to communicate with you more regularly. Thanks again for all your support. I could accomplish nothing without your support.

Brian Donlon

I hope these words of Brian's fill you with so much more than what the daily news brings, and that his words come to you today with my wishes of finding peace in our world. It is hard not think of our daily struggles a little differently when we hear of someone else having such a road to face each day and the gifts they give to each of us in the process.

To Your Successes and Victories…

Keeping the Faith

If you think you can win, you can win. Faith is necessary to victory.

~William Hazlitt

Happy Monday,

This morning, as I write these words onto paper, I carry with me a faith that all is well and right with the world. Does that mean that all is as good as it can be, or as perfect as it can be… well…? With Christmas Eve two weeks from today, I am aware of the fact that decorations still not in place, there are more presents to buy and wrap, more Christmas cards to be sent along their way, and many meals to be prepared.

But you know what I do have? The complete faith that it will get done as it needs to get done. It usually does – season after season, year after year. The truth is, if this is the worst trouble I have to deal with in my life, I am lucky indeed! Faith is such an important factor in looking towards our victories in life. This includes victories of all shapes and sizes, from watching our business and financial world succeed to nurturing our spiritual fortitude, health, well-being and our relationships with others.

Faith is an invisible ingredient that sometimes has no rhyme or reason. It just is.

Most people who find success in their lives do so with a strong faith in seeing what will come to be, as if it was already done. For me, the vision I see over the holidays is the ultimate moment when my family all sits down together at Christmas dinner. There is that special Christmas glow that falls over the table ultimately bonding us together in love and grace. This year holds a special excitement, as my Mom will be joining us at the table!

I wish you the faith in knowing you are on the path you need to be on and the courage to change direction if your faith is faltering. Things may not be perfect; you may have struggles, as we all do. Keep in mind, though, the challenges that are in our life are usually placed there to help us to see where we need to redirect our focus.

Today is the birthday of two very special people in my life (I've always inspired by the fact that they share a birthday). I want to wish them both a very Happy Birthday and a happy year ahead! To my sister, Robi, and my dear friend, Linda Lou – thoughts of you will be with me throughout the day.

Keep your faith – whatever that may look like – close to your heart. I hope these words of Norman Vincent Peale inspire you in the week ahead: "Believe in yourself! Have faith in your abilities! Without a humble but reasonable confidence in your own powers you cannot be successful or happy."

To Your Successes and Victories…

ACKNOWLEDGEMENTS

An expression of gratitude to those who have assisted along the way

Me, myself and I, we do nothing alone,
While living on a planet with millions
It is those who come into my atmosphere
Who make my world—complete.

With the final words of this book written, and the final editing done, there is nothing left to do except to launch this culmination of writings out into the world. But first come the thanks and acknowledgements that I would be remiss in not sharing.

The word namaste – meaning, "I bow to you" – at this moment in time flows into my mind. That word, along with the gesture of folded hands formed in prayer, with the eyes closed and body bowed, share a reference of common respect and honor. This is the thought and feeling that comes to my mind and my heart as I thank those whose contributions make the words of this book what they are today.

First of all, Namaste to you! It is my sincere hope that the words of this book will assist you in living with full appreciation for all the moments of your life. Remember that each one is special and brings something to your life in it's own unique way.

Namaste Napoleon Hill, for the brilliance of your words, ideas and ideals that have touched millions of lives – mine included. Though I was only 13 years old when you left this planet – your words lived on to mentor me towards my own destiny. My sincere hope is that my words will do the same for those who read them.

Namaste to the wonderful members of the Victory Circles, my Victory Sisters (and soon to be Brothers), each of you are an incredible inspiration to me as you move forward in making the dreams of your businesses a reality.

Namaste to the weekly readers and subscribers of the Victory Letters, your responses and feedback have inspired me to keep writing week in, week out – year in, year out.

Namaste to the many brilliant people whose quotes are used throughout this book, each of your words has inspired me to write and write and write some more.

Namaste to all the people mentioned in this book that are a part of my world, I couldn't have written it or lived my life as fully as I have, without each of you.

Namaste Maddy, Madeleine Hopkins of MN Hopkins Design, for the cover design and internal pictures of this book. You created exactly the perfect artwork

– as you always seem to have the knack of doing! You are such a blessing in my creative life.

Namaste to my editing team, which has included Suzannah Harris and my amazing assistant Melaina Daniel! And… I would be so remiss to not say a very special Namaste to Lise Amos who came in and did the final round of polishing edits. Lise, it's as if you were in my head prompting me to make the changes that were critical to fully get these words out into the world.

Namaste Janet Goldstein, for taking me under your wing and showing me the ropes and the to do's in getting this book out into the world.

Namaste to the many others who will assist in getting this book distributed and out to the world. They will be the ones who have made it possible for you to get this book into your hands.

And to my family who gives me the love and strength each day to do what I do:

Namaste Ed, my husband, as we move towards our 25th year of marriage together. You have been beside me allowing me to fully live my dream of being a writer and an entrepreneur – in the good and not so good times. Your support and belief in me is always propelling me forward. I can hardly wait for the years of play we have before us now that the nest has emptied. I love you!

Namaste Travis, my cherished son, my first-born. Our moments together I hope will last you a lifetime as you move into your role as an adult. You have greatness in you just waiting to be tapped into. Go forth and be great, knowing my love will always be here to support you along your way!

Namaste Bailey Jeann, my beautiful daughter, my precious Mammie. You are a special light in my life that I love and adore. I dedicated this book to you and Grandma because I see so much of her in you – both of you so strong in knowing what you want in life and then going for it. Now is the time for you to go out into the world and be all that you are meant to be.

Namaste to my siblings, as together we gain the strength to keep on going through this life together – especially now as we try to find our groove as the leaders of the family. Namaste as well for giving me such amazing nieces and nephews who I adore!

Finally, a special dose of gratitude and recognition for my mother – a woman that I had the blessing of 52 years of loving and being loved by on this earth. As I write these words she has been gone what seems like forever but in fact is now just about 18 months. We continue to feel her hovering around us – still making her presence known.

My mom's words, on the first page of this book came to me magically during one of her hovering moments I do believe. My sister, Robi, the consummate organizer (thank goodness for that) was going through some paperwork randomly when she came across this writing of Mom's. Two simple paragraphs that were written on a page of tablet paper, in my mom's special handwriting. I am so grateful to Robi for having the foresight and love to share these incredible words with us.

On the top of the paper above the words that you see at the very beginning of this book she had hand written: *Written June 30 1976 in Honolulu overlooking Waikiki Beach from the 21st floor of the Sheraton.* She signed her full name, Jeannine Landreau, at the bottom, in her beautiful, special handwriting.

Since finding it, I have imagined her sitting there as she overlooked the beauty of Hawaii, enjoying a cup of tea and savoring the moment. How appropriate that we would be given this gift after her departure from this planet. How appropriate that she would summarize perfectly the essence behind this, my second book, about finding the victories in all the moments of our life. It only saddens me that she did not get the opportunity to see our words together or to edit the words of this book as she did with my first.

Namaste Mom, for now giving me that ability to share your words next to mine.

Namaste Mom, for all the wonderful moments you have given me in my life.

ABOUT THE AUTHOR

Since the time she was a young child growing up in Southern California, **Cheri Ruskus** knew deep inside that she was destined to step up her game and help the underdog. Whether it was literally a pet in need or a friend who needed a shoulder, she was compelled to try to do what she could to ease their internal pain brought on by external conditions. Sometimes she thought that perhaps it was a curse because it tended to get her into hot water—more than once.

Today however, Cheri feels blessed to be looking at the world through her own pair of rose tinted glasses. For the past 30 years she has called Boulder, Colorado home and it's where her roots have been laid as an impassioned Entrepreneur. Cheri's key career focus has revolved around assisting entrepreneurs shoot past the barriers placed in front of them in order to achieve short term and long term success.

More recently, since 2006 and the inception of the Victory Circles, Master Mind forums for Entrepreneurs, Cheri has been primarily focused on insuring entrepreneurs have the tools and support necessary to take them towards long term profitability and sustainability.

The deep experience of 25 years of entrepreneurial successes and missteps that has taken her along her path was further deepened when Cheri became a Business Coach in 2000. She now shares her life experiences and entrepreneurial remedies with the Entrepreneurs of the Victory Circles.

The Victory Circles allowed Cheri to write a strong Master Mind curriculum paralleling some of the Master Mind principles for success that were originally written by Napoleon Hill in his epic classics, *Think and Grow Rich*, and *Laws of Success*. In fact, Cheri is so impassioned about these principles that she has written this, her second book from her experiences. Cheri's first book was written in 2001, *The Victory Letters: Inspiration for the Human Race.*

Cheri and her husband of twenty-five years are recent empty nesters discovering the possibilities of their second half of life with both of their children off to college.

Author Photo by www.lucytuckphotograpy.com

Printed in the USA
CPSIA information can be obtained
at www.ICGtesting.com
JSHW022215140824
68134JS00018B/1077

9 781614 480822